Lesbian and Gay Youth Issues

A Practical Guide for Youth Workers

by Gerald P. Mallon

CWLA Press • Washington, DC

CWLA Press is an imprint of the Child Welfare League of America. The Child Welfare League of America is the nation's oldest and largest membership-based child welfare organization. We are committed to engaging people everywhere in promoting the well-being of children, youth, and their families, and protecting every child from harm.

CHILD WELFARE LEAGUE OF AMERICA, INC.
HEADQUARTERS
440 First Street, NW, Third Floor, Washington, DC 20001-2085
E-mail: books@cwla.org

CURRENT PRINTING (last digit)
10 9 8 7 6 5 4 3 2 1

Cover design by Mary Flannery
Text design by Peggy Porter Tierney
Printed in the United States of America

ISBN # 0-87868-778-5

Library of Congress Cataloging-in-Publication Data
Mallon, Gerald P.
   Lesbian and gay youth issues: a practical guide for youth workers/
by Gerald P. Mallon
      p. cm.
   Includes bibliographical references.
   ISBN 0-87868-778-5
   1. Social work with gay youth. 2. Gay youth--Social conditions.
   3. Gay youth--Psychology. I. Title
   HV1426 .M34 2001
   362.7'086'640973--dc21   2001043543

Dedication

To Betsy Harris, with appreciation and love.

Contents

Acknowledgements

This book, unlike others I have written, was a labor of love and a pleasure to write because I could write without encumbrance on a topic about which I am passionate-gay, lesbian, bisexual, transgendered, and questioning (GLBTQ)* youth and their families. Moreover, because this is a book expressly for youth worker practitioners, I could write in a manner that liberated me from a traditional academic writing style.

I would like to thank several people for helping to make the writing of this book possible. First, I am grateful to the many fine colleagues with whom I have had the privilege of working over the years at the Child Welfare League of America (CWLA). The late David Liederman, former CWLA executive director, was a man who valued and respected the commitment that child welfare professionals must have for all children, youth, and families-including those who are not heterosexually oriented. He and his staff have always been supportive of my work with GLBTQ youth and their families. For that support, I am deeply grateful. I am also indebted to Robin Nixon, former CWLA director of youth services, who has been a close colleague and friend. Without her commitment to promoting youth workers' knowledge about GLBTQ youth and families, this book would never have been written.

My partner, Mike, and our boys, Ian and Travis, always deserve my full gratitude, as they are the most important people in my life. Their love sustains me and gives me the strength I need to continue doing the work I love to do.

I am also grateful to my many wonderful colleagues at Hunter College School of Social Work(in my view, one of the finest schools of social work in the country. Thank you for allowing me to be a member of your faculty and giving me a place to call home.

Special thanks go to my colleagues at Green Chimneys Children's Services, especially Betsy Harris for her loyal dedication. I am indebted to them beyond what words can adequately express.

Last, I want to express my appreciation to Joan O'Connell, administrative manager to the Executive Director of Green Chimneys Children's Services, who was my patient Microsoft Word tutor during the writing of this book. Her individual assistance and special knowledge made all the difference.

*For the purpose of brevity, the title of this book has been shortened to Lesbian and Gay Youth Issues. This volume, however, encompasses matters pertaining to all sexual minority youths-gay, lesbian, bisexual, transgendered, and questioning-abbreviated throughout as GLBTQ.

Preface

I have always enjoyed writing for practitioners because it is useful for real world workers, as opposed to my usual writing, which addresses an academic audience. In academic circles, writing aimed at practitioners is referred to as "practice wisdom." Practice wisdom is, at times, erroneously viewed by scholars as "too soft" and without rigor. I believe this perspective is deceptive. Practice wisdom is, in my opinion, one of the most powerful tools for teaching and sharing knowledge with fellow practitioners. It is a particularly potent form of knowledge generation when there is limited knowledge of the positivistic empirical variety, as is the case with respect to GLBTQ youth and their families.

Therefore, when Robin Nixon, former director of youth services with the Child Welfare League of America, asked me to write a practical guide for persons who work with GLBTQ youth, I was delighted to write from my heart, drawing on my 25 years of child welfare practice, and to share what I and others have found to be useful in our work with GLBTQ youth and their families.

What follows is a practical guide to help youth-service workers deal effectively with GLBTQ youth and their families in a variety of settings. It is written from a gay- and lesbian-affirming perspective that views homosexuality, from a nonjudgmental and amoral position, as a natural and normal variation of sexual orientation which is not pathologized. The data presented herein are practice-based evidence, representing the current thinking of leading experts practicing with GLBTQ youth and their families. The case examples used throughout represent actual GLBTQ youth with whom I have had the opportunity to work. These cases exemplify the actual experiences of youth in a wide variety of youth-service settings. I have gathered these examples as part of my work as a consultant, trainer, researcher, and practitioner throughout the United States and Canada. The names of these young people, and any identifiable agencies or geographic locations, were altered to protect their confidentiality.

Introduction

Preparing to Work with GLBTQ Youth

> I'm sure we must have some gay or lesbian youth in
> our program, but, come to think of it, I don't think that
> I have ever had any that have come out to me.
> —Training participant in a child welfare agency

This book is designed to help youth care providers increase their
knowledge and skills in working with gay, lesbian, bisexual,
transgendered, and questioning (GLBTQ) youth and their families. GLBTQ children, youth, and families affected by issues of
sexual orientation are present in every youth-service agency in
this country. However, because most professionals do not have
adequate knowledge about homosexual orientation, these persons
are often an invisible population. Consequently, most youth
workers (including supervisors, managers, and administrators),
unless they are gay or lesbian themselves or have a highly developed knowledge base about working with this population, are
completely unprepared to address or respond to the needs of these
youth and their families.

In an easy-to-read GLBTQ youth remain, for the most part, invisible
populations-as indicated by the quotation above-the reality is
that, if you are working with adolescents, you are already working
with GLBTQ youth. This book provides workers with accurate
information and case examples of GLBTQ youth and their
families.

In an easy-to-read question-and-answer format, the first chapter provides basic information about working with GLBTQ youth.
Chapter 2 focuses on the important issues surrounding the "coming out" process. Family issues are the central points in Chapter 3.
The fourth chapter examines discrimination and antigay violence
in the lives of GLBTQ youth. Creating healthy social environments

for GLBTQ youth is explored in Chapter 5. The developmental appropriateness of relationships and dating is reviewed in Chapter 6. Chapters 7, 8, and 9 discuss an array of specific, unique issues for GLBTQ youth and those who work with them in residential, school, health, and mental health settings. A Resource List of readings, videos, websites, and program services follows.

The programs featured throughout the book have been tested and are currently used across the country. Names of staff are not listed, however, because of possible staff turnover, changes in positions held, and variations in program services. The names and cities of individuals in case examples have been changed to protect their confidentiality.

The organizations in the Resource List have extensive experience in the field and serve as wonderful resources for youth workers involved with GLBTQ youth and their families.

1

The Basics

Can Youth Really Be Gay or Lesbian?

> If you are a teenager and you say that you're gay, you
> are told that you are not gay and that you're going
> through a phase because you are a teenager. Or you're
> told that you are mixed up and that once you come out
> of this stage (you know as a teenager you are supposed
> to go through these stages), then you will not be gay.
> That's their attitude! If we know that we are gay, they
> still tell us that we're not, it's just a phase. I think that
> they don't want to believe that young people can be
> gay. (Mallon, 1998, p. xx)

This quotation aptly expresses one young man's frustration in
getting adults to believe that he is gay. Youth workers can also
relate to this situation, as many have probably asked themselves
at one time or another, "Is this youth really gay? Is he or she just
going through a phase?"

Although many adolescents experiment with expressions of
sexual behavior, or verbalize confusion about their sexual identity, it is important to remember that sexual behavior alone does
not constitute a gay or lesbian identity. Some teens experiment
with same-gender sexual behavior, but others are very clear about
their orientation as gay, lesbian, bisexual, or transgendered (GLBT)[1]
individuals.

Society is gradually becoming more affirming about the experiences of GLBT persons, as evidenced by television shows like
"Ellen" and episodes portraying gay themes on poplar shows like

---

[1]GLBT refers to gay, lesbian, bisexual, or transgendered individuals
throughout. GLBTQ refers to gay, lesbian, bisexual, transgendered, or
questioning individuals. See Glossary for further definitions.

"Dawson's Creek," thus affording GLBT youth greater opportunities to see visible images of their lives. As a consequence, some GLBT youth are coming out at earlier ages.

It is possible for a youth to be sure of his or her orientation—indeed, some youth are clear about their identity as a GLBT individual as young as age 10.

It is also common for some youth to shift back and forth between identifying as gay, bisexual, heterosexual, and back again. Dealing with ambiguity of sexual identity makes many adults uncomfortable, but gaining greater comfort with this ambiguity is an issue that youth workers must face.

This book deals with some of the questions youth workers have about GLBTQ youth. In the absence of accurate information, many professionals rely on their own knowledge, which may be based mostly on stereotypes and myths. The following series of questions and answers about GLBTQ persons will aid in replacing erroneous assumptions with valid, accurate, and relevant information about GLBTQ youth.

How does an individual know if he or she is GLBT?

For the most part, a person's knowing whether he or she is GLBT is a matter of paying attention to one's feelings of attraction. It is very difficult for many people to be honest with themselves about same-gender attraction because society is, in general, so unaccepting of these feelings.

Some youth know that they are GLBT early in life, while others do not acknowledge these feelings until much later. Coming out, as we shall see in the next chapter, can occur at any time in life, not just during childhood or adolescence.

Can someone be GLBT without ever having had a homosexual experience or relationship?

Yes. In fact, many GLBTQ youth have never engaged in a sexual relationship with another person, yet they know that they are GLBT. Sexual orientation has more to do with internal feelings—one's sense of fit—rather than actual sexual experience.

Can someone have homosexual feelings and not be GLBT? (Can someone have heterosexual feelings and not be a heterosexual?)

Yes. Human sexuality is very complex and not easily separated into rigid categories. It is perfectly normal for a gay or lesbian person to be attracted to someone of the opposite gender, just as it is perfectly normal for a heterosexual person to have strong feelings for a person of the same gender. Although almost everyone experiences these feelings at one time or another, usually during adolescence, they can still be confusing. Many youth who are struggling with issues of sexual orientation will test their feelings with both males and females. Some youth workers think that calling yourself gay or lesbian is just a fad—in some colleges, the term L.U.G. (or Lesbian Until Graduation) is used to describe the same-gender relationships with which some women experiment. Again, it is important to remember that youth eventually will be who they are. Nothing that anyone says to encourage or dissuade them will change their natural sexual orientation. Sexuality and sexual/gender identity is a complicated arena. Therefore, youth workers must develop skills for dealing with the complexity and ambiguity of sexual identity.

If a person has a same-gender sexual experience, is that person gay or lesbian?

No. Being GLBTQ is not only about sexual behavior. The sexual aspect of a GLBTQ youth's life is, of course, important, but to focus exclusively on those aspects is a mistake. In fact, as described above, many GLBTQ youth who are dealing with issues of sexual orientation have never engaged in sexual behavior with either opposite- or same-gender individuals. Knowing that you are GLBT is primarily about one's sense of internal comfort and sense of "fit." One young man described it this way:

> When I was trying to figure things out about whether or not I was gay, I first dated girls, then boys, then girls again. Somewhere along the line, it just felt better with boys. I

don't mean the sex, because I was then—and still am—a virgin, but it's kind of like trying on a pair of gloves. You know…if you put the left glove on the right hand, it fits, but somehow it doesn't feel right. Then when you switch it to the right hand, where it belongs, you know that you have a good fit because it feels right. No one has to tell you that it feels right, because no one really knows except for you. That's what makes it hard. You have to do a lot of figuring it out all by yourself.

In working with GLBTQ youth, youth workers need to be clear, both for themselves and for the youth with whom they work, that sexual orientation and sexuality involve many aspects of identity and relationships that go beyond sexual behavior.

Many heterosexual persons have engaged in same-gender sexual behavior and vice versa. These experiences do not change anyone's core sexual orientation.

What is situational homosexuality?

In certain same-gender-only environments (e.g., group homes; large, congregate care child welfare placements; all-boy or all-girl boarding schools; prisons; some religious communities; and the military) individuals engage in same-gender sexual behavior. For these individuals, their sexual orientation remains the same— they are heterosexual and would choose an opposite-gender partner if given the opportunity. These individuals are sometimes erroneously labeled as bisexuals. Some may be questioning, but most are probably heterosexual.

How many GLBTQ persons are there?

Since most GLBTQ persons, especially youth, hide their true sexual orientation because of social stigmas, it is very difficult to ascertain how many GLBTQ persons there are. The commonly accepted figure is that 10% of the population, or 1 of 10 people, is GLBTQ. This estimate is based on studies conducted by researcher Alfred Kinsey in 1948 and 1953. No definitive study has been conducted more recently to confirm or refute Kinsey's findings.

Nevertheless, it is safe to say that, no matter how many GLBTQ persons there are, every youth service agency in the United States has some youth who identify as GLBTQ.

Have there always been GLBTQ persons?

Yes. Throughout history, evidence of homosexuality exists in art, literature, and music.

Can a person become GLBTQ?

No. A person cannot "become" GLBTQ, any more than a person becomes heterosexual. Since sexual identity comes from an internal sense of fit, most GLBTQ persons become aware of these feelings as they grow. Exactly where these feelings come from and why remains unknown.

Are some people born GLBT?

According to some researchers, preliminary evidence strongly suggests a genetic and biological basis for all sexual orientation. Although many gay males, some bisexuals, some transgendered persons, and some lesbians recall always knowing they were "different," others do not agree with the "gay from birth" philosophy. Again, research in this area is very limited.

Is being GLBT a choice?

Just as heterosexual people do not "choose" their sexual orientation, most GLBTQ persons do not choose theirs. The only real choice most GLBTQ persons have is whether or not to be open about their orientation. Some GLBTQ persons envision their entire identity as a social construction—a series of choices that one makes about constructing their lives. These people feel it is their choice, not society's choice, to determine what they do, including sexual orientation.

Can someone be seduced into being GLBTQ?

No. It is simply not possible for someone to be seduced into being gay, any more than a gay or lesbian person could be seduced into being heterosexual.

Do GLBTQ persons recruit others to become gay?

No. What sometimes happens, however, is that a youth who is struggling with issues of a GLBTQ identity meets another GLBTQ youth who is open about his or her identity. The struggling youth then realizes that he or she might be able to come out. Because there is strength in numbers, having a peer who is also GLBTQ can be a wonderful support system for someone who is internally struggling with the same issues. This occurrence might make someone believe that the "formerly heterosexual" youth was recruited, but that scenario is not possible or accurate.

Are GLBTQ persons more likely to molest a child?

No. According to researchers, the persons most likely to molest children are heterosexual males. Despite this clear evidence, many people continue to promote the myth that being a GLBTQ person is synonymous with being a child molester.

Is a GLBTQ person someone who was sexually abused as a child?

Although some GLBTQ people—just as some heterosexual people— were sexually abused as children, no evidence suggests that sexual abuse makes someone GLBT. We do know that sexual abuse can make a child very confused. Consequently, some youth who have experienced sexual abuse might be categorized as questioning.

Are people gay or lesbian because they have not met the right person of the opposite gender?

No. In fact, many gay men and lesbians have been partners of or married to opposite-gender individuals. Being gay or lesbian is not a matter of meeting the right person of the opposite gender. It is about finding the right internal sense of fit with a person, usually of the same gender.

Could gay or lesbian people be heterosexual if they tried?

Many gay and lesbian persons have tried to be heterosexual. Being gay or lesbian is so condemned in our society that many gay and lesbian people try to pretend to be heterosexual, at least for part of their lives. Some even try for a lifetime, never acting on or acknowledging their gay or lesbian feelings. Others find ways to adapt to their feelings through furtive relationships. Still others remain married for years but ultimately separate or divorce and seek same-gender relationships.

How can you tell if a person is gay or lesbian?

At one time, many people thought that gay and lesbian people were identifiable—through stereotypical mannerisms, affectations, dress, and so on—but the only real way to know if someone is gay or lesbian is if the person tells you. Too often, youth workers still look for the stereotypical nonconforming gender behaviors or mannerisms, but gay men and lesbians are very diverse, and stereotypes cannot confirm sexual orientation.

Are GLBTQ persons normal?

If normal implies being the majority, then the answer is no. Left-handed persons are also not in the majority, yet they are viewed as normal. Similarly, most GLBTQ persons view their sexual orientation as a normal variation of sexual orientation.

Is there a GLBTQ culture?

GLBTQ youth come from all races, cultures, ethnic backgrounds, religions, and social classes. Just as GLBTQ youth adopt the norms of their particular cultures, races, and classes as adolescents, GLBTQ youth also have vernacular, jokes, styles of dress, social events, and norms that are considered unique to their community. Because GLBTQ youth culture—like all youth culture—is regionalized, it is not possible to describe in detail all norms, styles, and social events, but youth workers should listen and look carefully for the terms and words that youth use with one another.

In large urban areas, particularly in the northeastern part of the United States—New York, Philadelphia, and Washington, DC—a popular social phenomenon for GLBTQ youth is known as the "ball scene." "Balls" are widely advertised and held in rented auditoriums or clubs, known as "houses." Headed by a "house mother" and "house father," youth attend to "walk the ball," competing in categories such as best face, best body, and best designer labels.

Some categories are funny, and some are serious. Competition is fierce, and winners receive trophies, but losers are "chopped." The ball scene is frequented by gay males, young lesbians, transgendered youth, and by some heterosexual youth as well.

Many GLBTQ youth also use slang terms for one another in a colloquial manner. Gay boys will sometimes jokingly call each other "girl" or "faggot," and lesbian girls will playfully call each other "butch" or "dyke." Some youth have also reclaimed the term "queer" as an inclusive term, stripping it of its hurtful intent and transforming it into a positive word. This is a generational term, because GBLTQ adults generally avoid it.

It is inappropriate for adults to use these terms with youth, as they are strictly "in-group" terms for youth to use with each another. But youth workers should listen carefully for all the terms that youth use. Because all slang varies geographically and changes rapidly, it is not possible to spell out all the slang terms GLBTQ people use with one another.

Despite many unique facets of GLBTQ culture, GLBTQ youth generally blend into the overall adolescent culture as much as any young person would, whether in rural, suburban, or urban areas.

Is there a GLBTQ lifestyle?

Most GLBTQ persons object to this term, because it trivializes their lives. If you are GLBTQ, you have a life, not a lifestyle. Just as there is no such thing as a heterosexual lifestyle, there is no such thing as a GLBTQ lifestyle.

Do gay men hate women, and do lesbians hate men?

Obvious tensions exist between the genders regardless of sexual orientation. In general, gay men do not hate women, and lesbians do not hate men.

Do gay men and lesbians hate heterosexuals?

Although some GLBTQ people have hostile feelings toward heterosexuals, generally no. GLBTQ persons have experienced some terrible things at the hands of heterosexual persons, but GLBTQ people also count many heterosexuals among their friends.

What is heterocentrism?

As explained briefly in the Glossary, heterocentrism is a result of heterosexual privilege and is analogous to racism, sexism, and other ideologies of oppression (Pharr, 1988). Heterocentrism most accurately describes the systemic display of discrimination against gay and lesbian people in major social institutions—in this case, organizations that serve youth. The primary assumption of heterocentrism is that the world is and should be heterosexual. This assumption, illustrated most clearly by heterosexual privilege, causes gay and lesbian individuals to engage in a constant search for a good fit between their individual nature, stigmatized by American society, and their environments, which are generally hostile and void of the emotional and psychological nurturing necessary for healthy growth.

The example below clearly illustrates heterocentrism in a family and the conflicts faced by a gay youth in the family.

> Victor, a 20-year-old gay Latino, lives in New York City with his father, Manuel, and his 16-year-old sister. Victor's father always reminds Victor of his "responsibility as a man." He talks to Victor about getting married and raising a family. Manuel is trying to be a good father, but he is unaware his son is gay. Victor dated a few girls in high school, but he began to understand himself as gay during his freshman year of college. Victor knows Manuel will have a difficult time accepting that his son is gay, so Victor has decided not to tell his father now. Victor is sad that Manuel has so many heterosexually oriented dreams for Victor's future—dreams Victor thinks will never be realized.

Why do so many people have trouble accepting GLBTQ persons?

Many people, including professionals, have trouble accepting GLBTQ persons for a number of reasons, but a primary reason is discomfort with the topic. In this society, people are uncomfortable with sexuality in general. Homosexuality seems to only exacerbate this discomfort. In addition, because American society traditionally is based on Judeo-Christian precepts, many people have religious perspectives that make it difficult for them to accept lesbian and gay persons. However, working with GLBTQ youth must be approached from an amoral—or nonmoral—objective viewpoint, without specific, personal moral or religious biases. Many people are uncomfortable dealing with GLBTQ because of these biases. Training and self-awareness sessions can help youth workers find ways to manage their anxieties and discomfort.

What is the best way to handle a sexual advance by a GLBTQ person?

A person's reaction to a homosexual advance should be the same as that toward a sexual advance from a heterosexual person. If the person is not interested, simply saying, "Thanks, but no thanks," is sufficient. If the person is interested, he or she can make that interest known. The exception, of course, is a client-staff situation. In such a case, the staff member is responsible for ethical behavior, which precludes any personal, physical, or romantic attachments with any clients he or she serves.

Staff Self-Awareness

One of the best ways to prepare for working with GLBTQ youth is to examine one's own personal issues regarding GLBTQ persons. Knowing the issues that trigger a personal, emotional reaction is crucial to good practice. Most people, including those who work with clients, have what I call "the big red button"—my visual metaphor for one or more personally sensitive issues that trigger an emotional reaction to others. Crucial to good practice is knowing what issues trigger a personal, emotional reaction. Although it is not always possible to avoid the issues that upset us when dealing with clients, it is both feasible and imperative to master one's reactions to the feelings triggered by sensitive issues. Openly acknowledging and addressing these issues personally, or with a supervisor or colleague, is a professional challenge. It is critical, however, to be self-reflective and work to develop a professional sense of self, including a heightened sense of self-awareness. As a practitioner working with a client, it is both unethical and ineffective to allow personal issues to cloud one's judgement.

The following guide[2] describes negative approaches that youth workers' sometimes use when dealing with GLBTQ youth, followed by more positive approaches that provide more effective service.

Negative Professional Approaches

Assessment

The youth worker or counselor

- believes that homosexuality is a disorder/pathology,
- automatically attributes problems to sexual orientation,
- discounts self-disclosure of sexual orientation as a stage or phase,
- fails to recognize heterocentrism or internalized homophobia,
- assumes heterosexuality,
- promotes the belief that homosexuality is a sin, or morally wrong.

Intervention

The youth worker or counselor

- irrelevantly focuses on sexual orientation,
- applies pressure to change sexual orientation,
- trivializes sexual orientation or experience,
- inappropriately transfers a client after the client's disclosure,
- allows personal beliefs to affect quality of interactions and unconditional positive regard of the client.

---

2. Adapted from Garnets, L., Hancock, K.A., Cochran, S.D., & Peplau, A. (1991). Issues in psychotherapy with lesbians and gay men: A survey of psychologists. *American Psychologist, 46,* 964–972.

Identity

The youth worker or counselor

- does not understand GLBTQ identity development,
- does not sufficiently take into account effects of his or her own internalized homophobia or that of the client,
- underestimates possible consequences of coming out.

Relationships

The youth worker or counselor

- underestimates the importance of intimate relation-ships,
- uses only a heterosexual frame of reference.

Family

The counselor or youth worker

- presumes that a gay/lesbian client is an inadequate parent,
- is insensitive to prejudice toward the experiences of gay/lesbian families,
- assumes that the family is in some way the cause of the youth's becoming gay/lesbian,
- assumes that only the gay/lesbian person, not the family as a whole, is affected by one person's disclo-sure.

Expertise and Training

The counselor or youth worker

- lacks expertise and relies on the client's knowledge about issues,
- teaches inaccurate information or discriminates against GLBTQ clients and/or trainees and colleagues.

Positive Professional Approaches

Assessment

The youth worker or counselor

- understands that gay or lesbian identity does not equal pathology,
- recognizes effects of societal heterocentrism,
- recognizes that sexual orientation is one of many attributes and does not assume sexual orientation is necessarily relevant to the client's problems,
- recognizes the unique concerns of gay/lesbian youth of color,
- recognizes issues relating to sexuality, sexual identity, or gender identity.

Intervention

The youth worker or counselor

- uses understanding of homophobia to guide therapy,
- recognizes effects of his or her own sexual orientation, attitudes, or lack of knowledge,
- does not engage in therapy strategies to change sexual orientation.

Identity

The counselor or youth worker

- assists the client in developing a positive gay/lesbian identity,
- is inclusive of the client's strengths related to her or his identity.

Relationships

The youth worker or counselor

- understands and validates the diversity of relationships,
- recognizes the importance of extended families and families of origin,
- recognizes the effects of prejudice and discrimination on relationships and parenting,
- recognizes that the family of origin may need education and support.

Expertise and Training

The youth worker or counselor

- knows needs and treatment issues,
- uses appropriate resources,
- educates trainees/colleagues and actively counters misunderstanding and discrimination.

2

The Coming-Out Process

Although GLBTQ persons come out to their families and friends for many reasons, they do so primarily because they want to be free to be themselves and to be honest with the people they trust and love. Also, it is exhausting and personally destructive to pretend to be someone one is not. Some GLBTQ people come out gradually, telling the most important people in their lives first, usually friends. Many GLBTQ people continue the coming-out process by telling family and coworkers. Coming out, however, is a continual process.

Coming out, especially for GLBTQ youth, is a liberating experience. It is like being free after a long imprisonment. Living in the closet is exhausting and scary, but many GLBTQ youth work hard to keep their secret. Watching everything they do and say is often the most difficult thing that many GLBTQ youth have to do. Some become experts at hiding, but at a great expense to their health and well-being.

> Nina, a 16-year-old white lesbian, lives with her mother and her two younger brothers. Nina has always known that she was "different." By the time she was 13, she knew she was attracted to girls. It took her a while to accept herself as a lesbian, because of all the terrible things she had heard people say about lesbians. Nina is not open with her mother about her sexual orientation, because she is afraid of her mother's reaction. She knows a couple of girls in school who identify themselves as bisexual, but she is very careful in whom she confides. Sometimes Nina feels stressed, because it is not easy to keep secret something that is so much a part of herself.

Young people who have feelings of attraction for the same gender—just as for the opposite gender—often become aware of these feelings during adolescence. For heterosexual adolescents, these feelings are reinforced by their families, society, culture, religion, and peers as a natural part of growing up. Boys are expected to have girlfriends and vice versa. These expectations are expressed in many ways from an early age. The experiences of GLBTQ youth in dealing with their first feelings of attraction to another person are quite different, however. Even before they become fully aware of their feelings, GLBTQ youth receive cultural messages that their feelings are not acceptable or normal.

> By the time I was 13 or so, I didn't have a name for what I felt, but I knew I was "different" somehow...I had brothers, and when I compared myself to them, I knew that I was different. My clearest memory is watching the TV show "Batman" after school one day. I looked at Robin's legs in his tights and thought, "He is so cute!" I knew other boys weren't thinking like that. While they were trying to imitate Batman and Robin's fighting moves...I was admiring Robin's muscular legs. That's when I first started to figure things out." —Kevin

This feeling of "differentness" is fairly common among gay and lesbian youth. Hearing other kids or family members use hurtful names about GLBTQ people reinforces the negative images that youth may have about themselves. Because of negative reinforcement, most GLBTQ youth hide their sexual orientation and pretend to be heterosexual.

Supporting GLBTQ Youth During the Coming-Out Process

Obviously, the ultimate goal for the coming-out process is for GLBTQ youth to feel comfortable enough with themselves and their orientation to make it known publicly. It is important to remember, however, that the goal of working with a GLBTQ youth is not to get him or her to come out to you, but to facilitate and support the experience of coming out, if and when a young person decides it is all right to do so. As with any situation involving youth, achieving this goal means establishing a rapport, trust, and comfort level with the youth. Practitioners working with GLBTQ youth have many ways to begin to establish this relationship.

- Use the words gay, lesbian, bisexual, transgender, and questioning. Use of these words, and the ability to say them with comfort, suggests to the client both a youth worker's comfort with these issues and a sense of safety in talking about these issues.

- Rather than looking only to the youth for gay/lesbian cues, indicate with your own cues that you are comfortable with issues of sexual orientation.

- Make sure your work place has some visible signs that it is all right to be a GLBTQ youth in your program. Posters, books on the bookshelves, and flyers on the bulletin board are all very useful and clear signs.

- Do not make or tolerate jokes or negative comments about anyone based on race, culture, national origin, gender, ability, age, religion, or sexual orientation.

- Provide all young people with opportunities to talk about sexuality in a healthy way, and be sure to include GLBTQ persons in those discussions.

- Help the organization and staff respond to the needs of GLBTQ youth by encouraging training, organizational reform, and review of policies that might discriminate against GLBTQ youth.

- Realize that GLBTQ youth have many more aspects than their sexual orientation. Like all young people, they need support, appropriate adult role models, care, concern, guidance, and flexibility.

Because of the stigma attached to gay and lesbian individuals in American culture, most gay and lesbian youth keep their orientation from their families, friends, and most youth service providers. This "invisibility" is a dominant feature among GLBTQ youth. It can make a service provider working with GLBTQ youth unsure about providing appropriate service, because no outward features identify a GLBTQ youth. GLBTQ youth remain invisible for many reasons:

- fear of rejection from friends and family members,
- fear of verbal harassment,
- fear of physical violence from others,
- fear of being treated differently,
- fear of being misunderstood,
- fear of being exclusively sexualized,
- fear of being perceived as sick, deviant, or sinful.

It is important to understand the reasons why GLBTQ youth hide their sexual orientation from others and the process by which they are socialized to do so.

Some GLBTQ youth, like Nina at the beginning of this chapter, repress their homosexual feelings and even monitor their behavior, hand movements, and styles of dress in an effort to stay invisible. This constant self-monitoring can cause many GLBTQ youth to experience stress that is devastating to their mental and physical well-being.

Aside from self-monitoring, some GLBTQ youth sublimate their homosexual feelings in other ways. Positive acts can include overinvolvement in sports, academics, extracurricular activities, or church groups. The youth may try to be exceptionally good at everything to cover up the part of them they think is bad. Negative acts include substance abuse or putting themselves in dangerous situations. Such methods may be effective in the short term, but the stress brought on by these types of sublimation prevents the healthy personal development of GLBTQ adolescents. The possibility of such destructive or unhealthy behaviors makes the practitioner's role with GLBTQ youth all the more important.

Roles and Responsibilities of Youth Workers During the Coming-Out Process

If a young person discloses, should professionals share it with coworkers?

In most cases, youth workers should not share this information with coworkers, but it depends on the circumstances. Factors to consider are whether all information about youth in a program is shared among staff, the degree of staff members' comfort levels regarding issues of sexual orientation, and whether a practitioner agree not to disclose the information. Youth should be encouraged to disclose when they feel safe and comfortable with others, but no one, including a youth worker, should ever disclose someone's sexual orientation to anyone without his or her permission. Disclosure is a very personal choice.

Should any of the disclosure/coming-out process be documented?

Documentation depends on the agreement that a worker makes with a youth at the time of disclosure and also on the guidelines set by agencies with respect to documenting of sensitive information.

Should practitioners maintain confidentiality?

Yes. Youth workers should never take it on themselves to "out" another person. As with any sensitive information related to a case, the youth worker should keep the information confidential unless the client gives permission to do otherwise.

How should youth workers handle a situation in which a GLBTQ youth is "found out" by a family member?

Unfortunately, not all GLBTQ persons are afforded the opportunity to come out on their own. Being "found out" refers to a situation in which a person does not have an option about coming out, such as a family member or friend learning about his or her sexual orientation inadvertently. In many families, this can cause a crisis.

I came home from school one day and found my mother
crying at the kitchen table. I ran to her and said, "Mommy,
what's the matter? What happened?" She didn't say
anything; she just handed me this letter that a boy in
school I liked had written to me. It was obviously not the
kind of letter that most boys write to one another. I had
hidden it in my dresser, but I guess she found it when she
was cleaning up. When I saw that letter, my heart sank. I
knew that things would never again be the same because
now she knew. I wasn't ready to tell her, but she knew.

—Anonymous

Because GLBTQ youth are stigmatized, and most adults view
youth through a lens of heterosexuality, youth workers' understanding of stigma is important. It is essential that youth workers
have an adequate grasp of GLBTQ identity issues before a crisis
occurs, because they may be called on to assist the youth and his
or her family in dealing with the issues related to being found out.

If a young person is found out by his or her family, the family
will need support, assistance, and compassionate understanding
from those persons trying to help them. Youth workers must be
prepared both to provide such support and to know other community resources available to the family. For example, youth workers
can provide support by supplying the youth and family members
with useful literature about sexual orientation issues, utilizing
crisis intervention strategies for families who may be prone to
verbal abuse or physical confrontations, or finding temporary safe
housing or permanent shelter for a youth who has been thrown out
of the family home. Being found out usually throws an entire
family unit—not just the GLBTQ youth—into a crisis. Most families need assistance to emerge intact from this crisis.

Stages of Development During the Coming-Out Process

It is important for youth workers to understand the psychological
stages that GLBTQ youth commonly go through during the com-

ing-out process. (The following information is based on the works of E. Coleman [1987], Vivienne C. Cass [1979], C. De Montefiores & S. J. Schultz [1978], and Richard R. Troiden [1993]). These stages describe a baseline of development of gay and lesbian sexual identity and an understanding of stages that GLBTQ youth may encounter during their development. As in all human behavior, many factors influence individuals' development, and most people do not pass through an orderly sequence of stages. Defining stages of human behavior provides only a basis for understanding, and progression through the stages is not limited to forward growth. Many life experiences influence the movement among the stages. Along with the description of each stage, suggestions are given for supportive actions useful in working with young people who are facing the experiences and difficult decisions related to these transitions.

Stage 1: Could I be homosexual?

Confused about self-image, youth may seek more information on homosexuality. Some theorists believe this is normal development for all youth. Negative reinforcements from society about homosexuality create more confusion about self-image, and youth often see no similarity between themselves and the public images and perceptions of GLBTQ persons. Youth workers should encourage youth to explore their feelings. Youth workers can also identify sources of accurate information on GLBTQ identity.

Stage 2: I might be gay/lesbian.

When youth accept this possibility, they may experience alienation, isolation, and loneliness. Heterosexual behavior learned previously has little or no significance. Youth cling to heterosexual behavior to maintain a public image and because they do not have access to alternative role models for sexual identity. Youth workers can provide accurate information and stress that GLBTQ identity can be a positive option. They may also recommend to the youth nonerotic novels with gay and lesbian characters. (For suggestions, see Books For and About GLBTQ Youth in the Resource List.)

Stage 3: I am probably gay/lesbian.

During this stage, alienation most likely is peaking. Youth are driven to seek out other GLBTQ persons in the broader culture. Their highest priority is finding a role model: someone by whom to gauge themselves. At this stage, a positive role model may lead to a positive self-image, whereas a negative role model or no role model may lead to further alienation. Practitioners can help youth to identify and can provide access to positive role models, such as gay/lesbian support or education groups.

Stage 4: I know I am gay/lesbian.

When youth achieve self-acceptance of their homosexual identity, sexual experimentation may follow. In general, youth are more concerned about whether they fit into their subculture than how they fit into American culture as a whole. This concern for peer approval can be difficult for any youth. If there is no obvious place for them in the GLBTQ subculture, most youth will temporarily end sexual identity formation and enter biphasal development, living a public heterosexual life while privately engaging in or fantasizing about gay or lesbian activity.

To circumvent this cessation of identity formation, youth workers can provide direct access to nonerotic GLBTQ youth organizations or service providers. The youth worker can also help the youth identify ways to come out that will build self-esteem. Strategies for coping with negative social reactions can also be identified. The youth worker also can build among adults in the general community an understanding of why disclosure is important.

In some cases, a youth may exhibit all of these behaviors but still avoid coming out. It is then incumbent on the youth worker to accept the youth's decision not to come out, while continuing to facilitate the process of disclosure if the youth wishes to do so in the future. A youth who exhibits behaviors of a GLBTQ youth, yet is refusing to come out, is probably at increased risk of engaging in high-risk and self-abusive behaviors. Youth workers should be continually empathetic and accepting, as this will undoubtedly be a difficult time for the young person.

Stage 5: I am a lesbian or gay. So what?

In this case, the person sees no clear dichotomy between hetero-sexual and homosexual worlds. The person is able to integrate homosexual identity into all aspects of life. This stage indicates a high level of maturity and a wide range of life experiences. Most youth have not yet achieved this stage. It is helpful to keep in mind that this stage is a goal to be achieved.

Conclusions

Finally, coming out is a distinctly GLBTQ phenomenon. Hetero-sexual youth do not have to deal with it. It is important to keep in mind that coming out is a process, not a one-time event. Coming out is a personal decision for each person who struggles with sexual identity issues, and youth workers should serve each GLBTQ youth as the unique person that he or she is.

10

3

Family Issues

Despite the great strides GLBTQ persons have made in society over the last three decades, coming out to their families and dealing with the issues that accompany disclosure remain very difficult tasks for most GLBTQ youth.

Families provide youth with economic, emotional, and social support. Family members are enormously important forces in a youth's life. How parents and other family members react to a lesbian daughter or a gay son can have a great impact on a youth's life. Parents' reactions usually depend on their culture, background, communities, racial group, and religious beliefs. Regardless of how open-minded parents are—for instance, they have gay or lesbian friends and are actively involved in civil rights issues—most parents are shocked and completely unprepared when they learn their son is gay or their daughter is a lesbian. Bisexual and transgendered youth usually face even more profound issues in dealing with their family members.

Helping Youth Decide

Before they can help the family of a GLBTQ youth adjust to disclosure, youth workers must first ensure that the youth is ready to disclose. Not all young people should be encouraged to disclose to their families. In some cases, disclosure is inadvisable. First, determine why the youth has decided to disclose at this particular time, and help the youth to anticipate the consequences of the disclosure.

The following suggestions for youth workers are designed both to assist youth in deciding whether to come out to their families and to support youth and families following disclosure.

- Ask the youth if any other family members are GLBTQ.

- Explore how open or closed the family system generally is to new ideas and new people.

- Ask how the family system has dealt previously with new and unexpected information. The response may provide insight into the family's flexibility and may assist in determining which family members will and will not be supportive.

- Ask the youth a series of questions: To whom do they feel closest? To whom have they confided before, and who has confided in them? Such exploration may help the individual to decide who might be the most supportive family member to disclose to initially, if the youth chooses to disclose. Who are the most liberal members of the family? Who will handle this information the best? How does the family grapevine work? Such exploration may help the youth decide who is the most supportive member of the family for initial disclosure. Genograms and eco-maps may also be useful tools in this process by helping the individual to depict family systems graphically. These tools allow for matter-of-fact questioning that can assist in gathering sensitive information.

- Role-play the disclosure process with the youth. Explore several perspectives with the client and offer feedback and suggestions on how the conversation can be accomplished smoothly.

- Help youth to see that coming out to family members is not a one-time situation but a process. Because individuals and their families disclose on a continuum, encourage a youth to consider disclosing first to a family member with whom he or she is emotionally close.

- Assist clients in developing a plan for orchestrating the disclosure to the entire family.

Supporting the Family Through the Coming-Out Process

Parents

Parents can experience a range of reactions, including shock, fear, guilt, shame, denial, disappointment, and sometimes anger and hostility. Many parents, relying on erroneous information they have heard, hope their child is only going through a phase. Others may wonder, "Did I do something wrong?" Some may express fear about AIDS, worry that they will never have grandchildren, or think that this is an attempt to punish them in some way. Many of their reactions have little to do with reality but are reactions based on stereotypes and myths about GLBTQ persons.

> Jose, a 17-year-old gay Latino, lives with his parents and two older brothers. Since he was 15, Jose has known that he is gay. He has not told his parents, although he did tell his brothers. After thinking about it for a long time, Jose decided that he wanted to tell his parents that he was gay. After dinner one night, he sat both of his parents down in the kitchen to talk to them. He said, "Mom, Dad, I love you both very much, and I want you to know who I really am. About two years ago, I came to realize that I am gay." His parents were stunned. His mother started to cry, and his father looked like he might cry also. Jose felt terrible, but he knew that he could no longer go on living with them and not tell them who he really was. After the initial shock of disclosure, Jose's parents calmed down, and his father said they would help him get therapy if that was what he needed. His mother nodded her head in agreement.

Many parents initially believe that their GLBTQ child needs therapy. Although this may be helpful for some GLBTQ youth and their families, it is not helpful for everyone. It is a common initial response, however, for many parents to immediately urge the young person to get therapy. Some parents, although upset at first about the disclosure, deal with it in a loving way. Other parents react harshly to a child's disclosure.

> Marianne is a 16-year-old lesbian. One evening, while she was talking to her girlfriend on the phone, unbeknownst to Marianne, her mother listened in on the extension to their entire conversation. After Marianne hung up, her mother confronted her. "Why was that girl talking to you like most girls would talk to a boyfriend?" Marianne tried to play it cool, but her mother persisted. "Are you gay?" Marianne did not know how to react, but her mother didn't give her a chance to think. Her mother grabbed her by the arm and threw her out of the house.

What is often hardest for the parents of a GLBTQ child is coping with the sense of embarrassment and shame about what friends, family members, or even strangers will think if they find out. Ironically, once the GLBTQ youth comes out, it is often the parents who find themselves in the closet, hiding the truth about their gay or lesbian child. They are asked frequently by others "Does your daughter have a boyfriend?" or "Is your son dating anyone?" Parents have to decide for themselves what to say to these and other awkward inquiries and comments from others. Youth workers should be aware of the common stages families of GLBTQ youth go through after disclosure, because these stages are just as important as the stages the individual youth goes through when coming out.

Although some evidence suggests that women tend to be more open-minded about sexual orientation issues than men are, not enough evidence exists to generalize that fathers always have more trouble with their gay sons or mothers always have more trouble with their lesbian daughters. It is probably accurate, however, that mothers and fathers have different expectations for their child(ren), depending on whether the child is a girl or a boy. Mario, in the case below, relates some of these parental expectations.

> My family is Italian, and when I came out to my father, he flipped. He said, "You're a man. I raised you to be a man.

What happened? Did I do something wrong? Didn't I take you to Little League and Midget Football? I can't believe this!" Somehow, he equated being gay to being less of a man. He got over it after a while, but I'll never forget his first reaction.

Families of color may have other issues with a child who comes out as gay or lesbian. Many families believe that dealing with prejudice about skin color or ethnic origin is hard enough. A young African American lesbian noted:

I told my grandmother that I was planning to come out, and she said, "Girl, you better go right back in. You are not coming out in this house—we have enough to deal with already."

Grandparents

"Whatever you do, don't tell your grandmother. It would kill her, and you're her favorite. She'll never need to know." These kinds of admonishments are frequently heard from well-intentioned family members. The truth is that grandparents are usually more accepting of their grandchildren than their own children. Grandparents also have knowledge of the family's history. One youth told this story about telling his grandmother that he was gay:

After I told her, she said: "You know, you're not the first family member who is gay." I was shocked; I couldn't think of who she meant. She said, "Remember your Aunt Libby and Aunt Pearl? Well, Aunt Pearl was your grandfather's sister, and Aunt Libby was her lady friend. We never really spoke about it, but they were gay." I couldn't believe what I was hearing, but it made me feel a lot better to know I wasn't the first.

Brothers and Sisters

Like parents and grandparents, siblings react in a variety of ways toward a gay or lesbian sibling's disclosure. Some are supportive, some are not. Some siblings may be fearful that their friends might think that they are also gay or lesbian. Others become advocates and champions of GLBTQ causes. However, one young woman commented on her sister's reaction to her coming out:

> One day my sister was really angry with me, and I couldn't figure out why. When I confronted her, she finally said, "You know, I know that you are very proud of being a lesbian, but I am not proud of it. You just keep coming out all over the place, and I get all of these looks in the hallway from everyone." I never realized what an impact my coming out had on my sister. I realized that I had to be more sensitive to her wishes as well.

What Can Youth Workers Do?

Youth workers can be of great assistance to both the family and the youth in this process. It is important for youth workers to be aware of the common stages families go through following disclosure of the GBLTQ identity of a son or daughter. These general stages and typical actions[1] for each are:

Finding Out

- emotional reactions
- cutting off the child
- conversion strategies
- denial
- acknowledgement

Communicating with Others

- telling friends
- learning from one's own gay or lesbian child(ren)

---

1. Adapted from Griffin, C. W., Wirth, M. J., & Wirth, A. G. (1986). *Beyond Acceptance: Parents of Lesbians and Gays Talk About Their Experiences.* Englewood Cliffs, NJ: Prentice-Hall; and Muller, A. (1987). *Parents Matter.* Tallahassee, FL: Naiad Press.

- learning from other GLBTQ persons
- learning from counselors
- learning from other parents

Changing Inner Perceptions

- opening up to feelings of grief, guilt, anger, failure, sadness, shame, loneliness, and fear
- moving toward acceptance

Telling Others

- coming out as parents
- speaking out in public
- educating critics
- allying with other parents

The Role of Youth Workers

Youth workers also can assist parents by becoming knowledgeable about appropriate stage-specific counseling interventions and the following support activities:

Finding Out

- reflecting emotional reactions
- increasing parents' range of affective responses
- avoiding collusion with bargaining
- challenging denial

Communicating with Others

- modifying parent's concept of homosexuality
- role-playing and rehearsing for telling others
- providing bibliotherapy (reading materials about GLBTQ persons)

- encouraging parents to overcome fear

Changing Inner Perspectives

- facilitating parents' progression through a sense of loss
- helping parents to recognize the effects of heterocentrism on children

Telling Others

- facilitating progressive disclosure
- helping parents move beyond fear
- role-playing with parents for public disclosures
- referring parents to Parents and Friends of Lesbians and Gays (PFLAG)

Finally, youth workers must realize that coming out will be a long-term process. Both the youth and his or her family may need to meet and to discuss these issues several times more in the future. It is important for the youth worker to provide support and meet with parents and other family members. The time immediately following disclosure is when they require the greatest amount of nurturance and support from both their child and the youth worker. Siblings also need assistance during this time and should not be neglected in the process. Encourage them to explore their feelings, provide them with information, and make them aware of support groups for families such as PFLAG.

4

Discrimination and Antigay Harassment and Violence

Many researchers who specialize in GLBTQ issues have suggested that the primary task of identity development for a GLBTQ youth is learning to manage a stigmatized identity. Unlike heterosexual youth, who are members of the dominant culture, GLBTQ youth must learn to manage their identity, which many still view as ignominious. Identity management essentially means deciding whom to tell—and not to tell—that one is gay. Although negative attitudes toward GLBTQ youth are slowly changing, discrimination toward GLBTQ youth still exists.

Discrimination

Although GLBTQ persons are protected by antidiscrimination laws in at least 10 states, many GLBTQ youth report experiencing discrimination in schools, foster care placements, employment, and the military. Discrimination is not always blatant; more often it comes in cloaked insidious ways: a vacancy in a group home is mysteriously filled when administrators hear the youth is gay, a school suddenly enforces its dress code when a lesbian dresses "too butch," a job becomes unavailable when the applicant is discovered to be a transgendered individual. GLBTQ youth of color are at even greater risk of discrimination—on multiple levels. To assist in protecting GLBTQ people, especially youth, from discrimination, several national professional organizations, such as the National Association of Social Workers, the American Psychological Association, and the American Psychiatric Association, have drafted statements about their policies on GLBTQ issues (see websites in the Resource List). One role of youth workers is to act as an advocate for equity, fair treatment, and justice when GLBTQ youth are targets of discrimination. Although advocacy is not always an easy role for youth workers,

it is an essential role for those concerned with the health and
well-being of all youth.

Antigay Harassment and Violence

Even worse than the experience of discrimination, GLBTQ youth
also often experience physical violence, solely because of their
sexual orientation. Pervaded by a heterocentric ideological system that denies, denigrates, and stigmatizes gays and lesbians,
American culture both attempts to make GLBTQ persons invisible
and then legitimizes hostility, discrimination, and even violence
against them. Unfortunately, physical safety has always been an
issue for GLBTQ persons. When GLBTQ youth engage in everyday
behaviors perceived as acceptable for heterosexual young people
(such as holding hands or kissing in public), they are accused of
flaunting their sexuality and are perceived as deserving of or even
asking for retribution, harassment, or assault.

    Therefore, it is not surprising that GLBTQ youth in various
studies report a high incidence of verbal harassment and physical
violence directed toward them because of their sexual orientation.
In one study of gay and lesbian youth in child welfare settings from
1994 to 1996 (Mallon, 1998), more than 70% of participants
reported being victims of physical violence because of their sexual
orientation; more than 90% reported verbal harassment. When
asked about the incidence of verbal harassment, one youth in the
study reported, "The name-calling was just a given. I almost didn't
even think to mention that, because it always happened. The
verbal harassment was regular."

    Others reported violence within families, schools, and com-
munities. A tirade from family members, peers, or even staff
members that might begin with verbal taunts and name-calling,
sometimes escalated into physical violence, including punches,
burnings, and rape. One youth worker recalled an incident of
community violence:

    One young boy was taunted and teased so badly in the
    community that he couldn't even go outside. The kids
    would just chase him. One man in the neighborhood

molested him. It was just horrible—very, very bad—and we had a lot of difficulty in the community. This child couldn't even live in the community in peace. We eventually had to move him for his own safety.

GLBTQ youth are often viewed as disposable individuals, deserving of being jostled or literally kept in the closet. Such youth have often found that typical youth-oriented environments are so poor and the fit so bad that they feel they have to flee for their lives.

Furthermore, the stigma attached to being a GLBTQ person often prevents youth from reporting their victimization, according to the 1994–1996 study cited above (Mallon, 1998). The youth say that when the abuse is reported, the victims are blamed. Consequently, of the youth who participated in the study, more than one-half chose, at some point, the perceived safety of the streets over the foster care system.

Identity management is closely linked to safety issues. When youth believe they are at risk for verbal harassment or physical violence if they come out or are found out, they are likely to hide their identity, if possible.

Even youth who are merely perceived to be GLBTQ are also at risk for verbal harassment or violence. The perception alone may be sufficient to provoke a violent reaction. Therefore, youth workers must also be aware of the dangers for youth perceived by others to be GLBTQ.

> Paul, a 16-year-old African American, has many mannerisms that are described by others as effeminate, but he identifies himself as heterosexual. He attends a local public high school and lives in a suburban community with his parents and three siblings. Paul has a good relationship with his parents and his siblings, but school has been a huge problem for him. He has experienced nearly constant verbal harassment because he is perceived to be gay. He was jumped in a bathroom by four boys who called him "faggot" and other slurs. He sustained multiple injuries and required a visit to the emergency room for treatment.

Because many people react in a hostile way toward GLBTQ youth or those who are perceived to be, safety is an important issue with which youth workers must grapple. Some professionals might suggest that not disclosing one's orientation is a practical solution. However, as shown in the above story, this solution is not always sufficient; perception alone may trigger a violence. Furthermore, nondisclosure places the burden of responsibility on the GLBTQ youth, not on those engaging in the verbal harassment or violent acts. Youth work professionals have the ethical and moral responsibility to create and maintain safe environments for every young person in their care. This safety is at the very core of all youth development practice. Listed below are several suggestions of ways youth workers can foster an attitude of tolerance and acceptance and help protect GLBTQ youth from antigay violence.

- Open a dialogue with all youth about accepting all forms of diversity.

- When discussing human sexuality with all youth, include content on GLBT experiences.

- Develop an antislur policy that protects all racial, cultural, religious, or sexual orientation groups.

- Adopt a zero-tolerance policy regarding all forms of violence.

- Post a list of rules and regulations that clearly state that all persons are respected and celebrated, regardless of race, religion, sexual orientation, culture, gender, and ability.

- Conduct open discussions with all youth about diversity in sexual orientation.

- Discuss gender-appropriate behaviors and mannerisms and why these do not indicate one's sexual orientation. Be sure to note cultural differences in norms of displaying physical affection, e.g., kissing on the cheek rather than shaking hands, touching during conversations, and clothing conventions.

- Maintain dialogues within and among organizations about the negative effects on all youth of discrimination and violence.

- Ensure that adults model appropriate acceptance behaviors for all youth.

- In the supervision and evaluation processes, make staff accountable for demonstrating their skills in creating a safe environment for all and their unconditional acceptance of all clients.

5

Creating Healthy, Affirming, and Safe Environments

All youth deserve support and an environment in which they are free to learn and to socialize with peers without fear of harassment or violence. Safe, supportive environments are essential for GLBTQ youth.

Although GLBTQ youth do not always require special services, they do require services that are responsive to their needs. GLBTQ and nongay youth can and should be integrated into existing youth services. In some circumstances, however, specific GLBTQ-affirming services should be created.

Determining Safety

GLBTQ youth become experts at determining whether or not their immediate environment is a safe one. They have to, because so much depends on it. GLBTQ persons constantly scan their environment to determine whether or not it is safe for them to be open about their sexual orientation. GLBTQ youth are, by definition, outsiders: outside the norm, the mainstream, different. No matter how integrated GLBTQ youth are into their families, community, school, they are still not part of the majority. GLBTQ youth are frequently fearful of being judged or discriminated against because they are GLBTQ.

Historically, GLBTQ youth have had to struggle to find their community. As GBLTQ youth begin to explore their identity, many believe that they are the only individuals who feel this way. Living in such a state of isolation can cause a young person to become depressed, anxious, and sad. At some point, when GLBTQ youth begin to realize that they are not the only GLBTQ people in the world, they have a strong desire to find others "like themselves." As one young person reported:

Before I came out, I really and truly believed that I was the only guy who liked other guys. There was no one in my school who I could identify as gay, and I certainly didn't know any adults who were gay—I felt so lonely. On top of everything, I couldn't talk to anybody about how I felt, not my friends, my family, anyone. When I finally figured out that there were others who were like me—I read this book called *Young, Gay, and Proud*—I couldn't wait to find them, but I had no idea where to begin looking for my kind.

Because GLBTQ youth have limited information about their own emerging identity, many embark on a quest to find "their kind." Until the last decade, many GLBTQ adults found their community in the gay and lesbian bar scene. Given the presence of alcohol and the fact that bars are adult environments, these are not appropriate settings for youth to meet others in their "tribe." Nevertheless, GLBTQ youth frequently find their way into GLBTQ bars. For many GLBTQ youth, these settings are their first introduction into the GLBTQ world. GLBTQ youth need to be able to socialize and meet peers in safe, healthy, nonerotic, alcohol-free settings.

What types of youth services do GLBTQ youth need? Basically, the same types of services that all youth need:

- community-based youth centers that affirm all youth
- drop-in centers where youth can hang out
- youth discussion groups
- afterschool programs for tutoring and studying
- recreational programs
- school-based extracurricular sports, music, and art activities
- service-oriented programs
- educational and instructional groups
- life skills groups
- counseling services

Generic Services Versus Special Services

Debate has occurred about whether to mainstream gay and lesbian young people into already existing youth services programs or to develop an array of specialized services for GLBTQ youth.

Opponents of special services note that GLBTQ youth need to interact within the larger heterosexual social context; they claim that separate programming promotes segregation rather than integration of GLBTQ youth.

Those who favor programs geared specifically for GLBTQ youth claim that GLBTQ youth will not use generic services, because they perceive these services as antigay. They also assert that special services are more likely to hire openly GLBTQ staff who, in turn, can empathize with the struggles of GLBTQ youth and act as role models. Proponents of specialized services note that youth services practitioners are often uncomfortable, unskilled, and untrained in working with gay and lesbian youth. Moreover, most youth services settings are generally unsafe places for a self-identified GLBTQ youth or even young persons perceived as gay or lesbian.

The best solution is a combination of both types of youth services. Services designed especially for GLBTQ youth can provide counseling and be sensitive to the issues important to GLBTQ youth in an atmosphere where they feel safe. Ideally, special services could refer GLBTQ youth to affirming agencies when required. For example GLBTQ youth requiring life skills training could participate in youth services programs with nongay youth. At the same time, however, generic services need to be able to respond to and create GLBTQ-affirming environments. In the final analysis, specialized services for GLBTQ youth would not be necessary if mainstream youth services agencies were held accountable for providing quality care to all children, including gay and lesbian children.

It is preferable for all youth to be integrated into appropriate services, but until youth services practitioners and their agencies become more knowledgeable and skilled in working with homosexually oriented adolescents, via training and technical assistance, specialized youth services programs are recommended.

Special programs provide both an array of youth service options and safe places for this underserved population of young people. Special environments for GLBTQ youth should be created when existing youth service environments do not provide for the safety and well-being of these youth. In some settings, GLBTQ are given clear messages that they are not welcome.

> Roberto, a 16-year-old Latino from Los Angeles, recounted his experience at a local community center. When he went to the local community center, all the other youth did was play basketball, but Roberto hates basketball. He tried to get involved with some of the youth activities, but he just didn't feel comfortable with all of those guys. He always felt they were looking at him and judging him. He heard about a youth group at the Lesbian and Gay Center in L.A. He was very scared to go there by himself, but one night he went to a meeting. "As soon as I walked in I thought—Thank God, there are other kids like me!" Finally, I could have some friends. Finding the youth group was the best thing that ever happened to me. I have friends, we hang out, sometimes we go to the center, sometimes we just do what other kids do—go to the mall, go to the movies—you know, just teenager stuff.

Although all youth service systems should have the goal of providing affirming, safe environments for all youth, providers must also understand that specific services make GLBTQ youth no longer feel like outsiders. These are places where they can be themselves. The stress of managing one's GLBTQ identity can be very tiring for a young person. Being able to let loose and just be themselves is very important for all youth. In a special environment, GLBTQ youth can be themselves, including being physically affectionate in a way that nongay and nonlesbian youth take for granted. Because GLBTQ youth experience stigmatization, they are sometimes unwelcome in existing youth services environments —or feel that they are unwelcome—because they do not find a niche in such a surrounding.

How can youth services agencies create environments that suggest safety and acceptance? On the basis of my own experiences in the field, I have developed the following 10 recommendations for developing an agency environment that is safe and affirms the identity of every young person:

1. Acknowledge that GLBTQ youth are among your clients. Do not assume that all your clients are heterosexual. The only way that anyone ever knows someone else's sexual orientation is if that individual tells you. Many times we make assumptions on the basis of inaccurate information or misperceptions. Just as clients will tell you who they are when, and if, they feel ready, GLBTQ clients will come out if and when they feel the environment is safe for disclosure of this information. Even if you think that you do not have GLBTQ youth in your organization, you probably do but do not know it.

2. Educate yourself and your coworkers about GLBTQ youth. Become familiar with the issues through the literature, bring in speakers, or ask an openly GLBT professional to act as a "cultural guide" to teach you and others in your agency about GLBTQ issues.

3. Use gender-neutral language. If a practitioner uses language that assumes a person is heterosexual (e.g., inquiring about a boy's girlfriend), a GLBTQ client may not feel that the professional is knowledgeable or comfortable about his or her sexual orientation and may not share valuable information. Use of words and terms such as "partner" or "someone special in your life" is appropriate, and it is important to use them.

4. Use the words "gay, lesbian, bisexual, transgendered, and questioning" in an appropriate context when talking with clients about diversity. Youth workers try to be inclusive by specifically referring to the diverse groups of people that we encounter, e.g., Latino, African American, Asian American, developmentally challenged. Being inclusive also means mentioning and acknowledging the existence of GLBTQ people.

5. Have visible cues in the waiting room or in your office that promote an affirmative environment for gays and

lesbians. Magazines, pamphlets, and posters with the words "gay" or "lesbian" or with recognizable symbols (see Glossary) printed on them let clients know that the agency is a sensitive, safe, welcoming place for them. If you put posters up and they are torn down—and they might be—put them up again and have a discussion about why some people react so strongly to these items.

6. Be prepared to change the culture of your organization. Condemning all slurs about any persons lets colleagues know that a joke is not funny if it is at the expense of any group. This sends an unambiguous message that oppression hurts everyone.

7. If a client discloses that he or she is GLBTQ, acknowledge it and talk about it. Don't just move on to other subjects. Use the disclosure for a deeper discussion. Talk about what it means to this client to be GLBTQ. Process the feelings with them. It is all right to let clients know that you may not be able to answer all of their questions or even to acknowledge that the subject makes you feel uncomfortable because you do not have a lot of information about what it is like to be gay or lesbian. It is critical, however, that, as a youth worker, you accept the person unconditionally, are supportive of the individual's struggle to come to terms with these complex issues, and are willing to listen.

8. Do not confuse transsexuality, transvestism, and homosexuality. Be aware that youth who are transsexual or transvestite are also members of sexual minority communities. They may or may not be gay or lesbian. They do, however, require services to meet their unique needs.

9. Research the resources that are available in the gay and lesbian community. Identify and become familiar with the resources for GLBTQ people in your geographic area (see the Resource List for suggestions). Visit the services available in your area, and explain your youth service program and your role in it. Be prepared and willing to

escort any clients who might be anxious or scared to a GLBTQ agency for the first time .

10. If you are gay or lesbian yourself, consider the value of your own coming out! Visibility is powerful, and GLBTQ youth can benefit from knowing youth workers who are open about their own sexual orientation. Heterosexual youth workers are expected to be candid about hetero-sexual issues. Of course, a practitioner does not have to be GLBT to work with GLBTQ youth. It is important to have role models that reflect the diversity of the youth, and nongay allies are also very important.

Systemic Responses: The Need for Alternatives and Strategies

To create consistently safe environments, system-wide policies and practices must be in place to support the individual responses described above.

Providing information, alone, is not sufficient. A system-wide recognition is needed that negative attitudes toward homo-sexuality and discrimination against GLBTQ youth contribute significantly to the difficulties that these youth encounter. Youth care professionals need to acknowledge the existence of young gay and lesbian people and develop ways to educate themselves, as well as the families of children in care, to understand the signifi-cance of sexual orientation in young peoples' lives and to help overcome the discrimination and oppression that contribute to the difficulties these youth encounter.

Support for youth and their families requires service providers who are trained in family systems and who are competent to address sexual orientation issues in a sensitive way. Part of the youth service provider's role is to increase the parents' knowledge about GLBTQ adolescents, as well as to model and encourage nonjudgmental and accepting attitudes and behavior toward the youth.

Providing youth services for GLBTQ youth can cause prob-lematic public relations concerns, particularly if the system does not have a clearly defined policy that includes proactively providing appropriate services for lesbian and gay youth. Youth services administrators would be wise to think about how to develop or adapt their program's existing services to ensure the safety of all program participants and how to deal with community attitudes that may be less than positive about GLBTQ issues.

Another strategy for creating safe environments can be found in transforming the youth services system into a unified service that is proactively responsive to the needs of lesbian and gay youth. Hiring openly gay and lesbian staff in community-based and residential programs is one step in this process. GLBTQ youth interviewed in several studies identified openly GLBTQ staff as instrumental in making them aware that the environment was safe. Closeted staff sent the clear message: "It's not safe for me to be out here—so it's not safe for you to be out either." For instance, Jane, from a major city, commented:

> When I walked into the center, I saw this woman who worked there....I recognized her from a dance I went to in the lesbian community. She looked really panicked when she saw me, and then she very much avoided me. In fact, she went out of her way to stay away from me while I was there. When I was leaving the center, she also walked out and said to me, "Please don't tell anyone, OK? I can't be out of my job." I couldn't believe it. I never went back there again. I mean, if the staff can't be open, then I knew I certainly couldn't be open.

Systematic, ongoing staff training and professional development for all levels of youth services personnel are also essential. Andres, a gay, 18-year-old African American from a midwestern city, commented about staff training:

> I don't know what they teach these staff in social work school or wherever they go, but they sure don't know anything about gay and lesbian people. I think they should all be required, before graduating, to take a Homosexuality 101 course—you know, a class to give them the language and to tell them about us. I am sometimes so shocked by how little the staff really knows about us.

Many still believe all of those old-time myths and stereotypes. It's amazing to me....

Because very few programs currently focus on meeting these
adolescents' needs, existing youth services programs particularly
need to be aware of the following underserved groups: adolescent
lesbians, transgender youth, gay and lesbian youth between the
ages of 12 and 15, and seriously emotionally impaired gay and
lesbian youths between the ages of 12 and 20. I am not suggesting
that specialized programs to meet these needs be developed by
agencies that serve youth. Rather, these youth are vulnerable
populations, within an already at-risk group, who may require
additional attention from youth workers.

6

Relationships and Dating

GLBTQ youth, like their heterosexual counterparts, enjoy developing relationships with peers. These relationships include dating and the development of romantic attachments. It is as natural for GLBTQ youth to date and to develop romantic attachments as it is for heterosexual youth. In fact, if GLBTQ youth are permitted to develop these age appropriate and developmentally appropriate relationships during adolescence, they will be less likely to have a biphasic adolescence later in their lives, and they will be more likely to develop fully as adults who envision and have healthy relationships in their lives.

GLBTQ youth, like all youth, want to be able to be involved in relationships. Like all youth, GLBTQ youth develop crushes, think a lot about boys or girls whom they like, and spend a great deal of time looking at and evaluating themselves to see how they compare with others.

Although online relationships are a poor substitute for actual face-to-face relationships, the Internet has made it possible for GLBTQ youth who have access to computers to socialize and meet other GLBTQ youth this way. This phenomenon has provided unprecedented opportunities for social interaction among GLBTQ persons. Depending on geographical area and/or the perceived need to hide, meeting other GLBTQ people can be a difficult prospect for some GLBTQ youth, particularly those in rural areas or small towns. In large urban areas, GLBTQ youth groups and gay/straight alliances in schools make it possible for youth to get together; in other localities, these opportunities do not exist.

Dating, it should be remembered, is a natural part of adolescence in this society. Not being able to date someone one likes, because of the stigma that is associated with a GLBTQ identity, can be very difficult for sexual minority youth.

GLBTQ youth frequently date persons of both genders, at least initially. Pedro, a young man in an urban area, commented:

First I dated girls, because that is what I thought I was supposed to do. I had a lot of friends who were girls anyway, so I went out with a few on dates—but there wasn't anything there. They were nice and all that, but there was no chemistry. After a while, when I got the courage, I went out with a few guys, and it was much better. There was something special there. But then I would date girls again, just to be sure that it was better with guys. It was kind of back and forth for a while. The whole dating thing was kind of like trying a glove on your left hand that is really meant for your right hand. It fits, but it doesn't feel right. When you switch it to the correct hand, you realize what a good fit really feels like.

Youth who have opportunities to date people to whom they are attracted will emerge as healthier adolescents and, later, adults. GLBTQ dating, however, makes many youth workers and other adults uncomfortable. This discomfort can be attributed to the following attitudes:

- Society's rejection of GLBTQ persons has been so strong that seeing GLBTQ persons in relationships can be disconcerting to many people.

- Youth workers may have internalized these negative images of GLBTQ persons to such an extent that, even as professionals, they think dating behavior is wrong.

- GLBTQ youth who hug, hold hands, or kiss in public are often perceived as "flaunting" their homosexuality, when in reality, they are behaving the same as teenagers who are heterosexually oriented.

- Youth workers may be nervous about a negative reaction from the members of the community. Youth workers should always set clear boundaries with youth. GLBTQ youth, like their heterosexual counterparts, can be very inappropriate in public because they are uncomfortable. Staff should model public behavior and set the tone.

Roles and Responsibilities of Youth Workers

Sexuality is a major aspect of adolescence. Becoming a sexual being is a major developmental task for all youth. All youth workers—and other adults—have varying degrees of comfort or discomfort with this topic. All youth workers must ask themselves, "How comfortable am I about discussions of sexuality and sexual behavior with any youth with whom I work?"

The first step in beginning to examine one's feelings about this topic is to be self-reflective on one's own values, attitudes, and feelings about all forms of sexuality. In some cases, youth workers will need to receive specialized training in human sexuality as it relates to adolescents. Dr. Michael Carrera, author of several books about human sexuality, provides a useful framework for setting in motion these discussions. (See the Resource List for citations.)

As part of this training, youth workers should be prepared to have open and accepting conversations with GLBTQ youth about topics such as dating, sex, love, marriage, commitment ceremonies, and rearing children. In essence, GLBTQ youth desire the same things as all youth. Youth workers should also try not to overreact to the fact that the discussions with GLBTQ youth will focus on same-gendered, rather than opposite-gendered expressions.

Avoiding Double Standards and Dehomosexualizing Behavior

Double Standards

If your organization has policies about youth who participate in your program and who are dating, it would be a good idea to make sure that these policies are gender neutral and that all young people are aware of them. Additionally, either ignore or enforce these policies evenly for both opposite-gender relationships and same-gender relationships.

Dehomosexualizing Behavior

In many cases, inappropriate behavior for opposite-gender couples is also inappropriate behavior for same-gender couples. Step back from the situation at hand and ask yourself, "If a boy and a girl were doing that, would I intervene? Would I stop them?" If your answer is yes, then it is probably appropriate to hold the same standard for a same-gender couple. If your answer is no, then deal with your own feelings and leave the youth to theirs. Consider, for example, the following situation:

> Two youth counselors in a community-based group home were summoned by the other residents to come outside to see what was happening. When they arrived, they witnessed two of the male residents engaging in simulated sex acts on the front lawn. Shocked at first by what they saw, the workers quickly assessed the situation and told the boys involved to come inside. They asked the other residents to go back to whatever they were doing. Although distressed by what the boys were doing on the group home's front lawn, they stepped back from the situation, dehomosexualized the behavior, and realized that if a boy and a girl were engaging in this type of behavior, they would know how to address it. They met with both boys, individually and privately first, and then together, to discuss why they were simulating sex. The counselors discussed with the boys typical adolescent sexual feelings and expressions of those feelings. The boys said that they were bored and were just "playing around." They said they were not involved with one another sexually, and they were aware of the house policy that prohibited sexual relationships between residents. The staff asked them not to "play" like that in public places—particularly in the front of the group

home, because they were concerned about being good neighbors. At the house community meeting later that evening, the issue was discussed, not as a means of belittling of the youth involved, but as a way to discuss the importance of appropriate behavior in the community.

In this situation, a potentially negative episode was turned into a teaching moment by staff who kept their cool and did not allow their own discomfort with the matter at hand to cloud their thinking.

GLBTQ youth have a right to have relationships, and, in fact, same-gender dating for GLBTQ youth is a healthy and natural part of their development. Despite the reality that this dating may make some youth workers uncomfortable, dating relationships should be nurtured and accepted as a part of the development of all youth.

7

School Issues

School and school-related activities comprise a major portion of an adolescent's life. GLBTQ students must cope with unique stresses that their non-gay counterparts do not have to face. These stresses, related in large part to their identity as a GLBTQ individual, may interfere with school socialization, school success, and the educational process itself. GLBTQ young people are often subject to verbal taunts and harassment directly linked to their sexual orientation. At times, the harassment escalates to physical violence, which can cause GLBTQ students to be truant or drop out all together. The example below illustrates the difficulties that some GLBTQ youth face in school settings:

> School was a living hell for me. It was "faggot" this and "faggot" that—all the time. It wore me out. I was exhausted from trying to watch my back and deal with all the verbal insults that were hurled at me. I finally couldn't take it anymore, and I just never went back. I took the GED and passed. That was the end of my high school career. It wasn't that I didn't like school—I just couldn't take the abuse anymore.

Schools can be very dangerous places for GLBTQ youth or even for those perceived to be, as shown in the next situation.

Simon, a 16-year-old, lived at home with both parents and two sisters. His family moved at midsemester of his junior year in high school on the East Coast. He recollected:

> At the new high school, they were all bullies. I was getting beat up all the time, just because they thought I was gay. I tried to keep a low profile, and one day this kid who had been bothering me all day just tried to jump me while I was in the gym. Then a whole bunch of other guys just started joining in, beating me, throwing stuff at me. I was

crying and screaming, "Why are you so bothered by me?"
It was so terrible, I just got to a point that I thought, "I'm
just not going to take it anymore. I can't keep going to that
school."

Although an honest and open discussion of homosexuality is
sure to evoke a great deal of discussion in any school setting, it is
important to remember that it is usually in school settings where
children first learn the power of the word "faggot." This unfortunate socialization process occurs in children as young as those in
kindergarten. If unchallenged by school authorities, its use continues through the high school years.

Because schools are the places where most youth spend the
majority of their waking time, schools are places that can greatly
influence the thinking of all youth. Not only are GLBTQ youth and
those perceived to be GLBTQ hurt by verbal epithets, but all youth
are affected by hurtful name-calling.

School-related personnel have an opportunity to stop verbal
harassment before it leads to violence, which often happens.
School administrators and school boards are becoming liable for
these issues when they fail to protect students from them (e.g.,
Jaime Nabozy was awarded $900,000 in punitive damages because
his school in Wisconsin did not protect him from injury). Therefore, school settings are now beginning to address ways that they
can intervene.

Although several schools in the United States are specifically
designed for GLBTQ youth, the solution is not to place all GLBTQ
youth in specialized schools (although some youth may need
that). Instead, all schools should be accountable for providing safe
educational environments for all youth to grow and thrive.

Making Schools Safe for Gay and Lesbian Youth, a report
published in 1993 by the Massachusetts Commission of Gay and
Lesbian Youth in School, outlines the problems faced by gay and
lesbian youth in schools and offers a series of recommendations to
guarantee safety and end abuse. Other schools interested in
providing more affirming approaches to educating GLBTQ youth
can replicate these recommendations. Information on obtaining a

free, complete copy of this report and others can be found online at http://www.magnet.state.ma.us/gcgly. Five of the report's recommendations, summarized below, can be used as a basis for creating gay- and lesbian-affirming environments in school systems.

1. Implement school policies that protect gay and lesbian students.

Professionals who operate in the absence of clearly stated policies utilize their own personal experiences as a guide. In dealing with homosexually oriented youth, this can lead to conclusions based on personal cultural, religious, and societal biases. Written, formal policies help prevent discrimination, harassment, and verbal abuse of gay and lesbian young people and those who are perceived to be gay or lesbian. Therefore, schools should establish policies to ensure equal access for all students to all courses and activities. Adopting and publicizing policies that ban antigay language and harassment on the part of the faculty and students are a simple straightforward solution, send a clear message to the school community, and cost nothing to implement. Obviously, violence of any type should not be tolerated, and clear procedures should be established to deal with such incidents.

2. Train teachers and counselors in the prevention of suicide and violence.

An essential component in creating safer environments for gay and lesbian students is to ensure that all school staff—teachers, administrators, cafeteria staff, maintenance staff, and support staff—are equipped with accurate and relevant knowledge necessary for addressing the needs of gay and lesbian young people in a caring and sensitive manner. In addition to training school personnel in violence prevention and crisis intervention, educational systems must also become expert in marshaling community resources to meet the needs of gay and lesbian students and their

families. Moreover, continued and ongoing education and training, for all levels of education professionals, are essential and
necessary to raise the consciousness about the need to develop
appropriate and safe environments for gay and lesbian youth. If
educators are truly committed to diversity, they must be willing to
address the issues of sexual diversity as well. The myths of child
molestation and "recruitment" of young people must also be
directly confronted to overcome obstacles to providing competent
services to young gays and lesbians and their families. Clinical
theories that view homosexuality in developmentally pejorative
terms and moralistic arguments must also be addressed so that
they can be defused and countered. Changes in teacher certifica-
tion requirements and school accreditation requirements should
also be considered.

3. Create school-based support groups for gay and straight students.

Young people respond best to other young people. Development
of weekly support groups for gay and lesbian adolescents and for
other students who want to talk about gay and lesbian issues is
beneficial. Heterosexual young people need opportunities to talk
openly with their peers who are gay, lesbian, or bisexual. Gay/
straight alliances are effective in-school support groups. Schools
need to commit resources to this effort by advertising the existence
of such a group and by appointing a faculty advisor to facilitate
this process with the students. Guidance counselors, nurses, and
school social workers are frequently among the first to address
issues of sexual orientation in school systems, so these professionals should receive special training to provide support and information for gay and lesbian youth and their families.

4. Provide information in school libraries for gay and lesbian adolescents.

Young people who are, or think they might be, gay or lesbian
frequently do not have access to accurate information about their

own identity. Young people who have questions about sexuality and sexual orientation need to have resources and information about gay and lesbian issues available and accessible in school libraries. Such information should include videos, books (especially those written by young people for young people—see the Resource List for suggestions), pamphlets, and other materials for use by students, teachers, and parents. Information that is specifically written for the parents of lesbian and gay youth is also important (see Resource List). Libraries can develop a reading list of books on gay and lesbian issues as well as periodically display these books and materials in a highly visible way. A well-researched local guide to gay and lesbian youth organizations and organizations that support family members should also be available.

5. Develop a curriculum that includes content about gay and lesbian people.

The classroom is the heart of the learning experience for students in educational systems. Therefore, discussion about gay and lesbian issues and recognition of the contributions of gay and lesbian people to history, literature, arts, science, and modern society should be integrated into all subject areas and departments in an age-appropriate fashion. To do this, educational systems must commit resources to examining current curriculum for bias, providing faculty development to assist teachers in developing competence in this area, and encouraging and supporting teachers who attend conferences that focus on gay and lesbian issues relevant to their subject areas.

Other Recommendations

To promote competence with respect to working with gay and lesbian students and their families, other recommendations are:

- Break the silence that surrounds issues of sexual orientation, and affirm all forms of diversity.
- Work toward making the environment a safe one for GLBTQ youth. Schools need to foster an environment

where name-calling and slurs of all types are unacceptable. Schools must have a zero tolerance policy for physical violence of all types. Administrators should address physical violence swiftly, placing the blame clearly on those perpetrating the violence, not on the GLBTQ youth for being "out" about their identity.

- Establish school environments where it is safe for GLBT adults to be as open about their orientation as it is for non-gay persons. Having GLBT adults who are role models will benefit all students, not just GLBTQ students.

- Involve parents as much as possible in discussions about sexuality and sexual identity issues. Parental education is a key factor in abolishing myths and stereotypes as well as an effective means to reduce the stigma associated with being GLBTQ.

- Through the schools, support gay/lesbian/straight alliances such as the Gay Lesbian Straight Educators Network (GLSEN) programs or Project 10 programs found across the country. (See the Resource List for contact information.)

- Press school boards and schools to set standards addressing GLBTQ issues. The stressful experiences encountered by many GLBTQ youth in educational settings are cumulative and detrimental to their educational performance and also to their self-esteem and sense of self-worth. Teachers, coaches, teachers' aides, social workers, guidance counselors, and administrators play key roles—whether in mitigating or exacerbating—the negative effects of the stressors associated with school life for many GLBTQ youth.

8

Health and Mental Health Issues

GLBTQ youth may have health and mental health needs that are unique to their status as sexual minority persons.

Health Care Issues

GLBTQ youth have several particular health-related issues: reproductive health and parenting, trauma and sexual assault, eating disorders, substance abuse, suicidal ideation, and sexually transmitted diseases. Access to preventive and restorative health care services may also pose special difficulties for these sexual minority youth. Significant social barriers exist regarding self-disclosure of sexual orientation and sexual behavior, and the reluctance of youth to disclose may impede the diagnosis and treatment of medical conditions. Additional barriers include costs, lack of available and adolescent-specific health. For GLBTQ runaway and homeless youth, the harsh reality and environmental consequences of living on the streets further compound the risks.

What specific health care problems exist for GLBT youth? The limited literature that is available suggests that the health care profiles for each group—gay, lesbian, bisexual, and transgender—differ significantly. Young lesbians frequently note the discomfort that they experience in seeking gynecological care, as suggested by this young woman's comments:

> Every time I went to the gynecologist, he always asked me if I was sexually active, and when I responded that I was, then he immediately asked what form of contraceptives I used. When told him "none," I got this big lecture about unplanned pregnancy and not getting pregnant. I never felt comfortable telling him that the form of sexuality that

I was engaged in, namely with another female, could not get me pregnant. I just didn't think he could handle it. I did have a lot of health care concerns, but usually I got so turned off by his assumption that I was straight, that I just clammed right up and stayed quiet.

Not all GLBTQ youth are sexually active, but some are. Additionally, research shows that most young lesbians have also been sexually active with males. Contrary to the popular myth that young lesbians do not become pregnant, many young lesbians who engage in sexual relationships with men do become pregnant. These young women need guidance and advice on reproductive health and parenting. Many youth providers who work with pregnant teen mothers assume that, because these young women are pregnant, they must be heterosexual. This is, however, an error in their professional practice. The same is true for gay young men who father children. Not all young people are heterosexual just because they have engaged in heterosexual sexual contact.

Gay males often report using sexual experiences as a means of learning about being gay. Therefore, sexually active gay males are at risk for a broad range of sexually transmitted diseases. Unprotected intercourse puts them at risk for HIV infection and other sexually transmitted diseases. Hepatitis A and B are readily sexually transmitted. Hepatitis C, however, is chiefly transmitted via contact with blood and less often through sexual contact.

Gay males who are concerned with body image may also be at risk for eating disorders. Such disorders do not seem to be an issue for young lesbians, despite the fact that the majority of eating disorders in adolescents are found among heterosexual females.

Substance abuse is another leading cause of health concerns for GLBTQ youth. The numbing effects of both alcohol and other substances can be effective means of anesthetizing oneself from feelings of isolation and vulnerability. GLBTQ youth abuse substances for the same reasons as their heterosexual counterparts: to self-medicate, to relieve tension, to increase feelings of self-esteem, to experiment, and to assert independence. They also may abuse substances to manage stigma and shame, to deny same-gender feelings, and in some cases to fit in with a peer group.

In addition, GLBTQ youth are at risk for violence, as noted in Chapter 4. They are frequently the victims of assault, including rape and sexual assault. More than half of all rape victims are adolescents. Most reported cases are women, but males are also victimized. Because transgender youth challenge societal norms of gender, they are at particularly high risk for sexual assault and violence. Youth workers should be aware that verbal harassment can escalate into physical violence. They should also speak openly with all youth about strategies to avoid or to deal with violence should it occur.

Transgender youth also have unique health-related concerns. Many face discrimination in health care settings because they are gender variant. Fearing rejection, ridicule, and harassment, many transgender youth will not seek the services of mainstream health care systems. Youth with gender-identity issues frequently experiment with hormones, usually obtained illegally on the streets. Injecting unprescribed hormones into an adolescent body is high-risk behavior in and of itself, but many persons also share needles, thus placing them at higher risk for transmission of HIV, hepatitis, and other diseases.

Although not all transgender persons opt for genital reassignment surgery, some do. Genital reassignment surgery is not an option during adolescence; however, medically supervised hormonal therapy and ongoing counseling are options that can and should be explored. Genital reassignment surgery is an extensive, complicated process that can only be undertaken after the individual is an adult and has been evaluated and received counseling by professionals specifically trained in this area.

As noted above, living on the streets puts the health of many GLBTQ youth at constant risk. First, runaway and homeless GLBTQ youths typically do not have ready access to health care that recognizes and addresses sexual concerns. Furthermore, street youth often suffer from upper respiratory infections, body and pubic lice, burns and other injuries, sexually transmitted diseases, dermatological problems, and mental health problems, in addition to the life-threatening consequences of HIV infection, substance abuse, and street violence. Extremes of temperatures, irregular sleep in exposed places, poor diet, propensity toward smoking cigarettes, and the lack of opportunities for regular showers or other hygiene are all factors that exacerbate these problems. Hunger is also a serious problem for street youth. Several studies from Seattle, Los Angeles, and New York have suggested that more than 50% of the runaway and homeless youth populations surveyed identified themselves as GLBTQ.

As noted above, despite myths to the contrary, many young lesbians engage in sexual relationships with males; these relationships often result in pregnancy. Pregnant teens who live on the street find their problems magnified. Prenatal care is lacking, and living on the street with a child is an onerous prospect.

Mental Health Issues

Although homosexuality was deleted from the American Psychiatric Association's Diagnostic and Statistical Assessment Manual (DSM) over 35 years ago, some mental health professionals still act as though a GLBTQ identity is curable. Indeed, some clinicians claim to be able to "cure" homosexuality through reparative or aversion therapies. Research has shown that these efforts have been unsuccessful. Although one's sexual behavior is changed, one's sense of internal goodness of fit remains gay or lesbian. Contemporary clinical approaches to working with GLBTQ youth do not attempt to change the young person's sexual orientation, but instead work with youth from a GLBTQ-affirming perspective.

Although some young people can truly be diagnosed with gender identity disorder—i.e., transgender youth—most gay, lesbian, and bisexual youth are comfortable with their gender as male or female but clearly identify themselves as gay, lesbian, or bisexual. Many inadequately trained mental health professionals erroneously use the diagnostic category of gender-identity disorder for a gay, lesbian, or bisexual youth.

Youth providers must understand that it is not because one is GLBTQ that mental health services are required. Rather, the stress inherent in living life as a stigmatized person is what causes many GLBTQ persons to seek mental health services. GLBTQ youth who seek care may actually be more resilient and have more effective coping skills than those who do not seek assistance. It is also important to note that youth may need mental health services as a result of childhood trauma and stresses or an organic impairment not related to their sexual orientation.

Mental health practitioners most often see GLBTQ youth for depression, anxiety, suicidal behavior, somatic disorders, and gender-identity issues. In addition, chronic stress from verbal harassment is a common theme identified by researchers who investigate the experiences of GLBTQ youth. Coming out to family, fearing being found out, negotiating safety, and managing one's GLBTQ identity are additional stressors that these youth face. These factors can contribute to erosion of a GLBTQ youth's sense self-esteem and confidence and can lead to a need for treatment. In addition, the need to hide distorts almost everything about the life of a young GLBTQ person, promotes dysfunction, and can cause a youth to seek help. The most frequently abused youth are transgender youth who do not or cannot meet traditional cultural definitions of masculinity or femininity.

Homeless GLBTQ youth are also at risk for severe mental health problems. Street youth suffer primarily from anxiety and depression. Many have also suffered from childhood sexual, physical, or emotional abuse, or other trauma related to family violence, as described by Sara, a 17-year-old white lesbian in Los Angeles:

> My family was always a mess. My mom's boyfriends were always disgusting. Most times they beat her; sometimes, they beat my brothers and me. One of them molested me for years, starting when I turned 11. I didn't tell my mother….She couldn't even help herself, so how was she going to help me? My life, from the time I was 5 until the time I left home at 15, was a nightmare. Believe it or not, running away from home was the best thing that I ever did. But I still have a lot of bad memories that haunt me about all the stuff that happened to me.

Depression

Depression is characterized by deep persistent sadness, lack of pleasure, and in some cases by helplessness and hopelessness. GLBTQ youth may feel isolated and unsure of their orientation, may be unable to identify others like them, and may feel they are the only one like this. Because they often cannot identify others, they feel something is wrong with them, and depression is fairly common. Depression also occurs with other symptoms such as anxiety, eating disorders, substance abuse, and chronic illness. Depression and substance abuse are also closely correlated with suicide attempts.

Suicide

Although suicide is the second leading cause of death in all youth ages 13 to 24, substantial evidence suggests that GLBTQ youth are at even greater risk for suicidality (see Remafedi [1994] and Ryan & Futterman [1998]). Therefore, youth workers should be prepared to assess an individual's risk for making a suicide attempt. Youth workers should be aware of the risk factors for suicide, including:

- History of previous suicide attempts
- History of substance abuse
- History of psychiatric diagnosis, especially depression and bipolar disorder; anxiety, conduct, and personality disorders
- A family history of suicide
- The suicide of a peer or a friend

Life events that involve shame or humiliation as well as arrests, assaults, or disciplinary incidents at school are typical events that may trigger suicide attempts in vulnerable youth.

Youth workers who are making an assessment of a youth's suicidal ideation should consider asking the following questions as a part of their assessment, being careful not to use a tone that implies suggestion:

- Have you ever felt so sad that you considered hurting yourself?

- Have you ever thought about suicide?

- How often—and how many times a day—do you think of suicide?

- Have you ever thought about how you might hurt or try to kill yourself?

- Do you have a plan for how you might kill yourself? What is it?

- Are you considering doing this now?

Youth who are deemed to be at risk for suicide will, at the very least, need supportive youth workers with whom they can talk. Staff will need to share this information with a supervisor and will be responsible for seeking appropriate referrals for the youth at community-based health clinics. In some cases, if the risk is believed to be high, the youth may require inpatient hospitalization to ensure a safe environment.

At times, the psychological stress, as described earlier in this chapter by a lesbian young woman, is more than many young people can endure. Some GLBTQ youth reportedly made suicide attempts to escape from the isolation and estrangement from their pain. One youth, Buzz, in Toronto, Ontario, recalled:

> I was high every day. My life was a mess, and I hated myself. I had nothing. I didn't have a family that cared for me. I didn't have a home. I didn't have anyone I thought I could go to. I tried to kill myself three times. They always tried at the shelter to give me a referral for counseling, but I never went. I never trusted them. Finally after a pretty serious suicide attempt (I sliced up my arm with a razor blade), I was hospitalized. When I was released from the hospital, they found me a good place to stay, and things have been better since then.

Psychiatric Hospitalizations

Some GLBTQ youth who suffer from severe psychiatric disorders may require psychiatric hospitalization. Historically, mental health inpatient settings have ignored sexual identity issues or, conversely, have inappropriately made them the focus of treatment. It is not uncommon to find mental health professionals who still view homosexuality as a psychopathology.

Many issues present a challenge to adolescent mental health treatment facilities, including the availability of mental health services appropriate for youth. Having a self-identified GLBTQ youth may cause quite a commotion among staff who are not used to these patients. When inpatient treatment is warranted, treatment providers should assess the facility's ability to appropriately treat a GLBTQ youth appropriately. This review should include an assessment of staff attitudes, therapeutic approaches, and past experiences in working with GLBTQ youth.

The National Center for Lesbian Rights in San Francisco has for many years coordinated a legal advocacy program for GLBTQ youth who have been institutionalized and been subjected to involuntary aversion therapy for sexual orientation. Transgender youth, as the next vignette suggests, may be at particular risk for hospitalization for nonconforming behavior for their gender.

> Janet, an 18-year-old self-identified transgender male-to-female youth, was hospitalized in a residential treatment center in Utah. She was confronted by mental health professionals and family who asked, "Why can't you be more like a boy?" Janet struggled to defend her identity as a female. Despite all clinical efforts, she was steadfast in maintaining her identity. After 6 months of treatment—all of which was unsuccessful at converting Janet from a female to a male—Janet was discharged on her 18th birthday.

Daphne Scholinski's memoir, *The Last Time I Wore a Dress* (1997), provides a more extended real-life illustration of the experience of forced hospitalization for nonconformity to assigned gender. (See Books For and About GLBTQ Youth in the Resource List for a complete citation.)

The following form is a sample used by a mental health provider assessment for sensitivity.

Organizational Assessment for Competent Practice with GLBTQ Youth

	Yes	No
Has the organization worked with GLBTQ clients in the past?	____	____
How often are GLBTQ youth seen at the organization	____	____
Are any openly GLBT staff employed by the organization?	____	____
Are providers familiar with the needs of GLBTQ youth?	____	____

Describe the organization's treatment philosophy for working with GLBTQ youth. _____

_____

_____

How often has the organization's staff had training, and of what type, in working with GLBTQ youth? _____

_____

_____

Does the organization have linkages with other GLBTQ youth organizations?	____	____
Do agency policies include GLBTQ youth?	____	____
Do agency brochures and outreach materials include GLBTQ youth?	____	____

9

Working with GLBTQ Youth in Residential Settings

Most GLBTQ young people are not placed in residential settings. In fact, the majority of GLBTQ youth live with their families and never reside in a group home or a shelter at all. Those who are in a residential setting are young people who have experienced difficulties with their family system to such a degree that they cannot or should not continue to live at home.

Although some GLBTQ youth are thrown out of their homes when they disclose their sexual identity or when they are "found out" by their families, not all then enter residential care because of issues directly related to their sexual orientation. Like their heterosexual counterparts, the majority of GLBTQ young people in residential care were placed there before or during the onset of adolescence for reasons such as: family disintegration, divorce, death or illness of a parent, parental substance abuse or alcoholism, or physical abuse and neglect.

Living apart from one's family is seldom easy. Residential systems have long been and continue to be an integral part of the continuum of youth services. The structure of the different types of residential programs varies widely, from small community-based group homes and short-term respite care, to shelter facilities, to large congregate care institutions that provide long-term or custodial care. All of these services share one common feature that is unique to residential treatment: they provide care on a 24 hours per day basis.

Most group homes and shelters are staffed by child care workers or counselors who are employed by an agency to work in shifts to cover the facility 24 hours a day. The child care workers in group home settings play a very important role in the lives of the young people in their care. Nevertheless, they are often the lowest paid of any workers in the youth services system and generally have the least education and training. The daily stress of working with adolescents in this setting, combined with the poor pay, makes it especially difficult for staff to be empathetic and compassionate in their dealings with the young people. These same factors also account for a typically high rate of staff turnover.

In addition, most group homes and shelters for adolescents focus on preparing these young people for independent living on or before their 18th or 21st birthday, depending on state laws. Some group homes are warm, loving, and accepting of diversity; some are unnurturing, cold, and rigid. GLBTQ young people have lived in and described both. Both good and bad experiences are described in the sections below.

GLBTQ Youth in Residential Settings

GLBTQ young people have always lived in North America's residential youth settings, but it has often been difficult for professionals to recognize their existence for three reasons: (1) many of these youths do not fit the nonconforming gender stereotypes that most practitioners associate with a gay or lesbian orientation, (2) GLBTQ young people are socialized to hide, and (3) the moralistic attitudes of many residential youth services professionals who are contemptuous of a homosexual orientation and refuse to acknowledge them. In addition, most professionals are completely lacking in knowledge about normal GLBTQ adolescent development. Many administrators of residential youth-services agencies are fearful that acknowledging a self-identified gay or lesbian young person in their program might be seen as "encouraging" or "promoting" homosexuality.

The end result is that GLBTQ youth often remain hidden and invisible in residential systems. If they do come out, they are not provided with the same quality of care that is extended to their heterosexual counterparts.

One gay young man's reflections about his placement experience represent the views of many and provide a framework for examining the salient features of this issue. Jose, a 17-year-old Latino gay male, resides in a group home in New York City.

I wasn't even sure that I was gay, but I knew that I liked guys. One day when I was talking on the phone to this guy that I liked, my mother overheard our conversation and figured out what was going on. She started screaming at me, telling me I was sick, that I was crazy, and saying that I needed some kind of help. I was upset, because she really caught me off guard. I wasn't ready to tell her anything about myself; she just found me out. After an hour of screaming, she calmed down and told me it was just a phase that I was going through. Things were tense that week. She didn't tell my stepfather. She was afraid of what might happen if she told him. He often lost his temper, and sometimes when he was angry, he would hit me. Toward the end of the week, my mother told me that she was sending me to the Dominican Republic for the summer. "There they will cure you," she said. I had no choice; I had to go.

When I returned in September, obviously I hadn't changed, but I lied and told her that I had. She realized after two weeks that I had not changed. Things just deteriorated from that point. Finally, the silent treatment really got to me, and I asked my mother to place me. I had some friends in a group home, and I thought maybe I'd be better there. Most kids do not ask their families to place them, but I did. I just couldn't take living at home anymore.

Once I was in placement, I thought it would be better, but it just got worse. I was scared to tell anyone that I was gay, because I saw how the gay kids got treated. If they even thought you were gay, you were treated badly. Gay kids were not treated equally; they were treated like they were not normal, not human. It was hell to live there. I felt like I was trapped in a cage. I had no one to talk to, and I wasn't happy.

It was like I was abnormal, like I didn't fit in the crowd. Most of the kids were pretty cruel to gay kids, but the staff ...they were worse. One night this group of kids ap-

proached me about having sex with them, but I told
them no. They were really aggressive and told me that
if I didn't give it up, they'd tell the staff that I approached them. Well, I didn't give it up, and they did
just what they said they'd do. They told staff that I had
made sexual advances toward them. The staff met with
me, and I told them what really happened, but they
didn't believe me. They said, "All you fags are just into
the same thing; we've seen this before."

The next day, the people from the city came and placed
me in another group home. That one was worse. I got
jumped by a couple of kids on the first night, and the staff
there wouldn't even talk to me. It was terrible there. I was
treated so badly, I would just go in my room and cry. One
day, after all the teasing and harassment, I just couldn't
take it anymore, and I complained to the social worker
who was kind of new herself. She said she understood,
and she eventually helped get me placed in another group
home, one that was gay friendly. This worker ended up
being the only person who was cool with me. Months
later, I figured out that she was gay, too.

This social worker always said she knew I was gay and
that I should come out, but I denied that I was. She tried
to reassure me that she could work with me, but I knew
better. I saw how they treated the kids who were openly
gay, and I saw how they treated me because they thought
I was gay. There was no way that I was going to confirm
it for them. I didn't want to reveal it to them, because I was
afraid of how they would treat me if they knew for sure.
She kept pressuring me, but I refused to tell her anything.
I always tried to act so straight to fit into their crowd—to
fit into what they did—but I couldn't.

One day—the day I told her I couldn't take it anymore—
my social worker told me about a place where I would feel
comfortable. She said it was a place for "people like me,"
a place where I would fit in. But even then, I kept denying

that I was gay. They scheduled a visit for me anyway. Even though they made it seem like I had a choice about whether to go there or not, I guess that they didn't really want me. I guess they wanted me out, so I was transferred to Green Chimneys, and I felt comfortable there right away.

Finally, I had people I could relate to, people to whom I could talk. When I first got here, I was so happy—they had this sign that said, "Here, we respect everyone! Regardless of race, religion, sexual orientation, culture, class, gender, and ability." I was so relieved; I didn't have to hide anything from anybody. I could dress the way I wanted to, I could walk the way I wanted to, I could be free, I didn't have to hide. I could be myself. It was the first time I ever felt that way.

Unfortunately, stories like Jose's are not uncommon. GLBTQ youth in residential care report both positive and negative responses to their sexual orientation, although the negative stories typically outweigh the positive. Several themes emerge from Jose's story. These themes, discussed below, are useful in understanding the experiences of GLBTQ youth in residential settings.

Invisibility and Hiding

GLBTQ youth in residential settings are frequently an invisible population. Administrators and staff convince themselves that no gay or lesbian young people are in their care. Some professional staff and administrators associate homosexuality with gender nonconformity; they believe that they would be able to identify the GLBTQ clients if there were any. Only individuals who do not conform to traditional gender stereotypes (i.e., the "butch" girl or the effeminate boy) are identified as gay or lesbian and are then treated with disdain. The majority of GLBTQ young people, however, are silent, hidden witnesses to the negative attitudes of staff, administrators, and peers toward those who are believed by workers to be gay or lesbian. Thus, most GLBTQ young people in residential settings receive—from multiple sources—the message: "Stay in the closet! We do not want to deal with this!"

Stress and Isolation

Living in the closet, as so many GLBTQ young people in foster care do, is the source of a high level of stress and isolation in their lives. The comments of Brenda, a 20-year-old lesbian from Los Angeles, exemplifies these issues:

> I tried to hide it, because I saw how they treated those kids they thought were gay or lesbian. I mean, they were treated terribly—just because the others thought they were gay. I knew that I was gay, so imagine how they would treat me if they ever found out. I felt so alone, so isolated, like no one ever knew the real me. I couldn't talk to anybody about who I was. It was a horrible experience. Trying to hide who you really are is very difficult and exhausting. Sometimes I felt so bad, I just wanted to kill myself.

Multiple Placements

Moving from one's family to a residential setting is, in and of itself, stressful. Subsequent moves from one placement to another have been identified as a major difficulty for youth in residential settings. The constant challenge of adapting to a new environment is unsettling, provokes anxiety, and undermines one's sense of permanence. Other adolescents in residential settings move from setting to setting because of individual behavioral problems. Usually, however, GLBTQ youth report that their sexual orientation leads to their multiple and unstable placements, primarily for four reasons:

- The youth are not accepted because staff members have difficulties dealing with the youths' sexual orientation.

- Because of their sexual orientation, youth feel unsafe and either run away from the placement for their own safety or request another placement.

- If GLBTQ youth are open about their sexual orientation, staff perceive these youth as a "management problem."

- The youth are not accepted by peers due to their sexual orientation.

Andrea, an 18-year-old white lesbian from New York, describes many of these points:

> I couldn't live at home with my mother, because she couldn't deal with the fact that I was a lesbian. I currently live at a shelter for runaway and homeless youth. First, I was placed in a diagnostic center, but I left there after about 10 minutes, when I could tell that they couldn't deal with my orientation. I went AWOL from there and stayed at my friend's house. They didn't say anything about my being a lesbian, but it was obvious that they had a problem with me. If I felt that people couldn't deal with me, I just ran away. I mean my feeling was, I couldn't live at home because my mother couldn't deal with it, and if the staff in the group home can't deal with it either, then why bother sticking around? After that, I went back to my mother, then to a couple of group homes, then to the place where I am now.

Many agencies simply get rid of GLBTQ youngsters because staff cannot deal with the youths' sexual orientation. Many of these youth have been put in multiple placements by agencies at all levels of care. Wilem, a 19-year-old Latino from New York, provides an account that is representative of many young people's stories:

> I have had so many [placements]...Too many to remember, all of those overnights... a lot of places. I was 14 when I went to my first one, but I kept running away because I just couldn't live there. I was even running away from home, because I didn't want anyone to know that I was gay. Some were good...the worst wasn't horrible, but it still wasn't the best place to be. I stayed at one place for a while because I met some gays there that I knew from outside, so we hung out together and they showed me the ropes.

These case examples exemplify the ways in which GLBTQ youth are continually faced with having to negotiate new environments, many of which are inhospitable and lacking in the conditions, staff, and programs necessary for healthy psychological development.

Replacement and Feelings of Rejection

The majority of GLBTQ youth sense they are not welcome in most residential settings. They perceive that they are accepted reluctantly into some placements. Consequently, they feel isolated and have negative reactions to their residential settings. Many young people are impassioned about their maltreatment in these settings, as Wilem notes:

> How was I treated? You mean the way we were treated? It sucks. I mean I wouldn't want to go back to one. It's hard enough being in a situation when you are away from your family and then having somebody else put you down...I mean, it's just not fair.

Some young people report that they left their placement once they realized that they were not welcome. For instance, Maura vividly recalls:

> As soon as I get discriminated against, I leave. When I was on a psychiatric ward they were trying to give me aversion therapy. I mean, they were supposed to help me with my depression, not by telling me that I'm wrong. Where I am now, they are fine, but in other places, there were definitely problems. In one place, they were giving me my own room because I was gay and to keep the other kids away from me. It's the kids and the staff who treat you differently.

Frequently, young people who leave placements become lost in the system, as their multiple placements create a sense of impermanence and drift.

Verbal Harassment and Physical Violence

Many young people enter residential placements because they offer sanctuary from abusive family relationships and violence in their homes. With the constant threat of harassment and violence within the system, GLBTQ youth report being unable to feel completely secure or confident. Although violence and harassment may be an unfortunate component of residential care from time to time for all youth, GLBTQ young people, unlike their heterosexual counterparts, are targeted for attack specifically because of their sexual orientation. One transgender youth recalled the nightmare of verbal harassment and physical violence in this narrative:

> I was coming home to the shelter one night from my job, and I was just minding my own business when these three boys from the shelter started to yell at me, "Hey, you she-male, what are you anyway, a guy or a girl?" I tried to ignore them and walked a bit faster to get to the shelter, but they kept following me—taunting me, embarrassing me in front of all these people on the street. I felt so humiliated, so bad, so low. Finally, one of them jumped me from behind, pulled up my skirt, and tried to sexually assault me with his fingers. That's when someone stopped their car and yelled at them to stop. They ran, and this guy got out of his car and asked if I was all right. I said I was, because I was embarrassed and humiliated—but I was hurt inside more than outside. I didn't go back to the shelter that night or any other night. I had some money, so I rented a cheap room for the night, and then I went to stay with friends. It was a terrible experience, but I never reported it. I figured no one would do anything about it.

Creating Safe Environments: Individual Responses

Professionals faced with these harsh realities might well ask, what can be done? The most important response to such an inquiry is the reminder that all professionals in youth services have the ethical and moral responsibility to create and maintain safe environments for every young person in their care. The establishment of such safety is at the very core of all youth-services practice. Specific suggestions are listed in Chapter 5.

Conclusions

The problems encountered by GLBTQ adolescents and their families are frequently ignored and largely unrecognized by the majority of youth-services professionals, just as the youth-services system has been deficient in addressing the specific needs of diverse ethic and racial minorities. Crucial to the recognition of and response to the needs of this population is an understanding of the impact of societal stigmatization of GLBTQ individuals and their families.

Effecting changes in attitudes and beliefs, in pursuit of competent practice with GLBTQ adolescents and their families, requires education, training, and self-exploration on both the individual and the institutional level. The development of competence in this area holds promise for preserving and supporting families and for the establishment of appropriate residential services that are affirmative for these GLBTQ young people and their families.

10

Conclusion: A Call for Organizational Transformation

Over the past few years, several authors have addressed the needs of GLBTQ youth and have identified obstacles that youth-serving agencies face in meeting those needs. Using the experiences of several agencies that are nationally known for affirming GLBTQ youth, this chapter offers recommendations on agency philosophies concerning the reality of GLBTQ youth and their needs, as well as suggestions on ways to create safe, welcoming, and nurturing environments.

The dilemmas faced by GLBTQ youth and their families are clear. Youth-serving agencies, already challenged by many substantive issues, tend to exhibit a range of sensitivities to GLBTQ youth. At one extreme, some agencies openly discriminate against GLBTQ youth. At the other extreme, others are affirming in their approaches and strongly advocate for the needs of GLBTG youth. Most youth-serving agencies are somewhere between the two extremes. Many agencies initiate good faith efforts to become more affirming, usually when they encounter their first openly gay youth. A more proactive stance and preparation for working with diverse groups of youth rarely happens without a precipitating incident.

Youth-serving agencies come into contact with GLBTQ youth because of family conflict, the health or mental health of the youth, school problems, or out-of-home placements. The scope of these issues, as noted earlier in this book, requires that all youth-serving agencies be knowledgeable about and sensitive to the needs of GLBTQ youth. The vulnerability of GLBTQ youth, particularly at times when they come to the attention of youth-serving agencies, is yet another reason that youth service providers should be prepared for working with this population. The most inopportune time to increase one's knowledge about a service population is when they arrive at the agency in a crisis and need immediate assistance.

Efforts to increase sensitivity to GLBTQ youth cannot be sustained in an environment that does not explicitly encourage such undertakings. As agencies struggle to demonstrate their commitment to diversity, they must also be willing to include sexual orientation in that diversity continuum. In doing so, they begin the work necessary for creating a safe and welcoming environment for all clients, not just GLBTQ youth. Once this environment is established and the organization's culture shifts to clearly include GLBTQ concerns, it becomes possible for youth workers to learn about, advocate for, and provide affirming services to GLBTQ youth.

While it is a reality that some agency administrators and boards might object to sensitivity awareness or programs specifically related to the GLBTQ population, fewer individuals will take exception to broader approaches designed to increase worker competence in working with all clients who are underserved.

Transforming the Organization's Culture

Transformation is a powerful word, but nothing less is needed to create programs that are responsive to the needs of GLBTQ youth. Appreciation of diversity is a key element in this process. The examination of an organization's commitment to diversity is a common theme for all youth-serving agency administrators. Organizations have used various strategies to address diversity and to increase worker competence in meeting the needs of a varied client population. These strategies may include in-service training, nondiscrimination policies, culturally specific celebrations, advocacy, client/staff groups that explore diversity, and efforts to encourage a climate that welcomes all people. An approach that is appropriate for GLBTQ persons could be integrated into any one of these areas. For example, a community-based youth center that celebrates Latino History month with a potluck dinner of dishes from various Latino countries might also celebrate Pride month by inviting a speaker to discuss the events that led to the civil rights struggle for GLBTQ persons.

Second, youth-oriented agencies must be committed to creating a safe environment for all youth. A zero-tolerance policy for violence, weapons, emotional maltreatment, slurs of all types, and direct or indirect mistreatment conveys to all clients that their safety is a priority. A strong stance against violence of all types, including verbal harassment, sends an important message to all youth. It says, "We will try to protect you, and you will not be blamed for being yourself. Those who offend are the ones who will be dealt with, because their behavior is unjustified and unacceptable."

Third, all youth benefit from youth workers who are open, honest, and genuine. Everyone benefits from philosophies that indicate an agency's willingness to address head-on the difficult issues. Giving clients and staff permission to raise controversial topics signals that all people associated with the agency will be treated with respect and dignity.

Only through intentional and deliberate organizational cultural shifts—true transformation—can a climate supportive of GLBTQ youth be developed. Several agencies across the United States and Canada have successfully created organizations where GLBTQ youth are welcomed, feel safe, and have their needs met. These programs do not require large amounts of money, tremendous time commitments by staff, or other extraordinary efforts. Such transformation does, however, take commitment from board members, administrators, and other key organizational players, including the youth and their families. The next section describes strategies that can be used to achieve these results.

Concrete Strategies

Hiring Supportive Employees

An organization that is responsive to the needs of GLBTQ youth must be staffed and administered by people who demonstrate commitment to providing services that foster self-esteem and acceptance of GLBTQ youth. To achieve this goal, the organization must aim to hire open-minded, supportive employees, including openly gay, lesbian, bisexual, and transgendered professionals. Organizations must communicate antidiscimination policies in hiring and be honest about recruiting and maintaining GLBT employees. Hiring openly GLBT employees sends a clear message demonstrating the agency's commitment to GLBTQ youth. Although hiring GLBT staff is a critical factor, it should not be assumed that every GLBT person is knowledgeable about working with GLBTQ youth or is an appropriate person to work with youth. All staff, regardless of sexual orientation, should be assessed for their appropriateness in working with youth and should be educated about GLBTQ youth, the problems they experience in society, and ways to support them effectively. Hiring non-GLBTQ staff who are comfortable with GLBTQ staff and clients and open to being educated about working with this population is essential to this process.

With increasing openness about sexual orientation, clients often ask employees about their sexual orientation. One agency, Green Chimneys in New York City, has encouraged staff to be open about their gender orientation. Previously, ambiguity about staff members' orientation led to mistrust by the youth. Once staff orientations were clarified, residents stopped their guessing games and participated more fully in the agency programs.

Several agencies have reported that one of the most positive outcomes of recruiting openly GLBT staff is that the staff turnover rate is at an all-time low. Employment in an accepting atmosphere is a valuable employee benefit for GLBT persons.

In-Service Training

In-service training that is integrated into the overall training efforts of the organization—not just one-shot deals—is critical in providing quality services to GLBTQ youth and families. As with all diversity issues, integrating real-life case examples into the training sessions can make the educational process come alive for workers. Good places to start are by helping staff identify appropriate language, eliminate common myths and stereotypes about

GLBTQ persons, replace the myths with accurate information about the population, and create environments that suggest safety. Specific training efforts should also be tailored to meet the individual needs of staff members from various disciplines.

Other critical factors in the training process are helping staff identify resources in the community and assess their own personal heterocentrism. Use of videos and guest speakers, especially GLBTQ youth and their parents, can be particularly effective in these areas.

Practice is needed to transfer abstract information learned in training sessions into actual intervention techniques. Participation in a variety of exercises assists staff members in beginning to develop a set of appropriate and unconstrained responses. Staff members can be intentionally exposed to situations that lead to self-reflection. For instance, in one training that focused on the maladaptive coping responses that can be associated with hiding one's sexual orientation, participants were asked at the start of the session to write their most personal secret on a slip of paper, to fold it, and place it under the chair where they would be sitting all day. Without participants ever being asked to share what they wrote, the message of the "hidden secret" was powerful. In the ensuing discussion, attitudinal change and understanding of the consequences of secrecy began to evolve.

Providing staff who attend the training with written information, resources, and other materials ensures that the educational process will continue after the training session is finished. Program supervisory staff should monitor and evaluate this ongoing process.

Welcoming Strategies

The creation of a physical environment that welcomes GLBTQ youth, families, and prospective employees is as significant as staff training. Again, these efforts do not need to cost a great deal of money, but their existence signals acceptance and safety.

The organization's waiting room is a very important place to start this process. Reading materials, symbols, and signs that specifically spell out the organization's attitude about respect for all people will be noticed and will help clients, their families, and employment applicants feel welcome.

Many agencies have posters hung in their waiting rooms that signal acceptance. For example, Green Chimneys Children's Services specifically developed nine colorful, gender-neutral posters that announce a GLBTQ-affirming environment through intentionally subtle messages. Few materials are specifically produced for GLBTQ youth, but one resource is Green Chimneys. GLBTQ organizations can provide organizations with pamphlets. Other information and graphics can be downloaded from the Internet. (See the Resource List for contact information and other resources.)

The presence or lack of books focusing on GLBTQ issues conveys important messages. For an extensive list of books on a variety of topics, see the Resource List. Numerous books related to GLBTQ topics are also available for purchase online.

Integrated Policies and Public Information Materials

An organization's commitment to GLBTQ youth involves much more than posters and books. It is essential to recognize that the internal structure of the organization, as reflected in its policies and public information materials, also needs to be evaluated. Training and educational efforts may assist staff in developing their competence in working with a particular population, but policies and community perceptions of the organization may also need to be altered to effect real change.

Although GLBTQ persons have experienced greater acceptance and understanding in the past 30 years, many organizations still actively discriminate against GLBTQ youth. In some cases, the organization's inattentiveness to the needs of GLBTQ youth will send a clear signal that they are not welcome. A review of an organization's policies and public materials can assist the organization in attempting to consistently provide sensitive services to all youth.

Advocacy Efforts

Recognizing that the environment outside the organization is often actively hostile to GLBTQ youth, agencies that serve youth must also be committed to external change and advocacy efforts. These efforts might include, for instance, participation in an advocacy campaign to end discriminatory language in contracts and in human services-related conferences. Affirming organizations must also be prepared to advocate for GLBTQ youth in community schools, in local adolescent treatment settings, and in families. Furthermore, organizational leaders must be prepared to work to educate local and state politicians and funding agencies about the needs of GLBTQ youth.

In this new century, youth workers continue to play a critical role in developing young people. Historically, youth work has had a cyclical interest in certain subjects, such as youth suicide, violence, substance abuse, and homelessness. All are worthwhile issues that require our best efforts, but the needs of GLBTQ youth should not be viewed as an "issue du jour" of youth work. Sexual orientation issues are too vital to continue to be overlooked. A particular gay or lesbian client might trigger a plethora of attention at one time, only to have the issue fade from view when the next issue presents itself. Dealing with GLBTQ youth issues in an intermittent manner is a mistake. Organizations must continue to develop diligently in training, in assessing their own ability or inability to respond to the needs of GLBTQ youth, and in addressing new approaches to competent practice with these youth and their families. For an organization to be consistently sensitive to the needs of its clients, efforts must be undertaken to create affirming environments and to transform existing ones. If all organizations are guided by the same principles that embrace diversity and can translate these principles into concrete action, GLBTQ youth will be better served.

Glossary of Terms Commonly Used in Addressing GLBTQ Issues

In working with any youth-oriented group, an ability to speak the youths' own unique language and to understand their culture is essential. GLBTQ youth have their own unique language. This language makes many adults uncomfortable, but to be effective in working with GLBTQ youth, adults must overcome their discomfort and become familiar with the terms that GLBTQ youth use to define themselves. Key terms listed below will assist you in this process.

The following glossary is intended to orient the reader to commonly used vocabulary in GLBTQ literature, culture, and speech. Language can be a source of confusion and misinformation. Therefore, it is important that service providers have accurate definitions. Heterosexually oriented care providers are often uncomfortable with the vernacular of the gay and lesbian culture. It should also be recognized that, as with any subculture-particularly with youth-there is constantly changing argot. Usage of glossary terms may vary by age cohort, demographics, geographic area, socioeconomic status, or cultural background. The most commonly used terms are listed first.

General Terms

Sexual Orientation

This is the commonly accepted, scientific term for the direction of sexual attraction, emotional and/or physical attraction, and its expression. Examples of sexual orientation are heterosexuality, homosexuality, and bisexuality. The term "sexual preference" is often used to express sexual orientation. Sexual preference, however, is also misinterpreted to mean that sexual attraction, including same-sex attraction, is generally a matter of conscious choice. Although such a choice might be possible, current research by scientists, such as Simon Le Vay (see Resource List), strongly suggests that sexual orientation is not a matter of choice. Thus, sexual orientation is the more accurate term. Sexual preference, sexual proclivity, sexual tendency, or the notion of turning gay or lesbian by choice are all inaccurate characterizations.

Heterosexual

This term refers to a person whose sexual attraction, both physical and affectional, is primarily directed toward persons of the opposite gender.

Homosexual

This term refers to a person whose sexual attraction, both physical and affectional, is primarily directed toward persons of the same gender. More preferable terms used to describe persons of this sexual orientation include gay and lesbian (see below).

Bisexual

A bisexual person is attracted to, and may form sexual and affectionate relationships with, persons of the same and opposite gender, although not necessarily at the same time. This term may be used to refer to sociopolitical identity, sexual behavior, or both. Bisexuality is a normal variation of sexual orientation, but the term can also be used as a transitional term by people who are coming out. Some adolescents will identify themselves as bisexual before identifying themselves as gay or lesbian, because bisexuality represents a mediating position between homosexual and heterosexual in traditional American culture.

General Usage for Heterosexual, Homosexual, and Bisexual

Except for strictly scientific or scholarly uses, it is inappropriate to apply the terms heterosexual, homosexual, and bisexual to individuals. Incorrectly used, those terms imply that sexual orientation is the sole basis of personal or group identity. For example, a gay, lesbian, or bisexual person may have ethnic, gender, regional, political, professional, and religious identities in addi-

Glossary   91

tion to his or her sexual identity. The term "homosexual" has been popularly misinterpreted as applying only to men. This use is also inappropriate because of its formal, clinical tone. It is generally advisable, therefore, to use the terms gay and/or lesbian when referring to people of homosexual orientation.

Gay

Gay refers to a person (either man or woman) whose homosexual orientation is self-defined, affirmed, or acknowledged as such. Gay also refers to homosexually oriented ideas (e.g., literature or values). It is believed that this term originated as a kind of code among homosexual men and women. It is a popular alternative to "homosexual" primarily because it is "our" word. It is a way for homosexuals to communicate among and about themselves with pride.

Lesbian

A lesbian is a woman whose homosexual orientation is self-defined, affirmed, or acknowledged as such. Lesbian also refers to female homosexually oriented ideas, communities, or varieties of cultural expression. The word lesbian historically refers to the island of Lesbos, where the poet Sappho and her female followers lived during the 6th century BC

General Usage for Gay and Lesbian

The terms lesbian/gay usually indicate a personal or social identity, suggesting that the person has identified herself or himself as lesbian or gay, or that a group accepts or affirms the identification (e.g., Gay Pride). The terms gay/lesbian are not necessarily synonymous with "homosexual." Individuals can be homosexual or have engaged in homosexual activities without identifying themselves as lesbian or gay. These latter terms have cultural and social connotations in addition to the sexual ones. A lesbian or gay person views herself or himself as homosexually oriented along with other aspects of personal identity (e.g., Italian-American Catholic athlete from New York). As indicated above, the term gay can refer to both men and women with a homosexual orientation, and some women accept and use the term. Other women, however, prefer the term lesbian because of its clear reference to women only. For practical purposes and for clarity, it is generally advisable to use the term lesbian when referring to specifically to homosexual women, and to use the terms "gay and lesbian" or "lesbian and gay" when referring to both genders. Such terms as "gay people" and "gay community" are often used to refer to both women and men of homosexual orientation.

Women-Identified Women

This term indicates women who have strong emotional ties and associations and who seek women as the most important members of their personal support system.

Questioning

This term is often used to refer to young people in three distinct aspects:

1. Questioning youth may be exploring issues of sexual orientation in their lives. Although many gay and lesbian adolescents are certain about their orientation, others are not as sure and may take time to explore their identity. Some of these young people will ultimately identify themselves as gay, lesbian, or bisexual; others will self-identify as heterosexual.

2. Youth who have been sexually abused and have not received treatment for their sexual abuse may question their sexual orientation. This is particularly true for youth who have experienced same-gender sexual abuse.

3. Youth with character disorders or severe psychiatric illness may, in an attempt to fit in, claim a gay or lesbian sexual identity that is not authentic.

Cross-Dressing

This term refers to the practice of dressing in the clothing commonly associated with the opposite gender. Cross-dressing is sometimes referred to as nonconforming gender behavior. A popular cross-dressing entertainment personality, for example, is the male supermodel Ru Paul. Not all gay males or lesbians engage in cross-dressing, nor does cross-dressing necessarily indicate one's sexual orientation (e.g., athlete Dennis Rodman). In earlier times, some women cross-dressed as men in order to gain the social privileges accorded to men (e.g., women who dressed as men to enlist in the armed forces; British author George Eliot (1819-1880), who was born Mary Ann Evans).

Transvestite

Individuals who wear clothing usually worn by persons of the opposite sex are referred to as transvestites. Some transvestites are heterosexual married men who cross-dress in the privacy of their homes for sexual or psychological gratification. Some gay men cross-dress in public; this is known as dressing "in drag." These men are referred to as "drag queens." Some, but not all, drag queens identify themselves as gay; many identify themselves as heterosexual. Transvestites are not to be confused with female impersonators. Female impersonators are men who earn a living by cross-dressing and performing as women, in night clubs, for instance. In some other times and cultures, the norm has been for men to dress as women in theater roles (e.g., in Shakespeare's time in England, in Japanese traditional Noh and Kabuki dramas). On occasion, impersonation of the opposite gender is undertaken for personal reasons (e.g., the play M. Butterfly, based on a real story of a man married to a female impersonator).

Transsexual/Transgender

Both terms encompass a variety of gender expression, including drag queens and kings, bigenders, crossdressers, transgenderists, and transsexuals. Some individuals cluster together to form their own communities and find their own gender identity-the sense of self as male or female-that is in conflict with their anatomical gender. Some transsexuals may live part-time in their self-identified gender; others desire to live fully in their self-identified gender. Some transsexual or transgendered individuals report feeling trapped in the wrong body. Some of these persons eventually opt for sexual reassignment surgery, a long, medically supervised process that also requires psychological testing and counseling to address issues of gender dysphoria. Most transsexuals identify themselves as heterosexual, not gay or lesbian. Some adolescents who feel trapped in the wrong body illegally obtain male or female hormones and attempt to intensify or change their gender. Although the drugs used are somewhat common on the streets, this practice is dangerous and poses several health risks, including possible HIV exposure through sharing or reusing needles if the drugs are injected.

Coming Out

Coming out is defined as "the developmental process through which gay and lesbian people recognize their sexual orientation and integrate this knowledge into their personal and social lives," (DeMonteflores & Schultz, 1978, p. 59). It can also mean disclosure, as in, "I just came out to my parents." "Coming out" is the process of first recognizing and acknowledging nonheterosexual orientation to oneself and then disclosing it to others. This process usually occurs in stages and is a nonlinear process. Thus, an individual may be "out" in some situations or to certain family members and associates but not to others.

The Coming-Out Process

Coming out is the process of first recognizing and acknowledging homosexual orientation to oneself, then disclosing it to others. This usually occurs in stages and is a nonlinear process. An individual may be "out" in some situations, such as among family members or associates, but not in others. Some may never "come out" to anyone other than themselves. Coming out is a process, and each individual needs to proceed at his or her own pace. This process is defined in greater detail in Chapter 2.

Coming out is a unique and very personal process for each person. Antigay and lesbian sentiment is so prevalent in American society that many GLBTQ persons remain closeted for various reasons. Youth of color, disabled youth, and immigrant youth who are also GLBTQ live with the dual tensions associated with coming out and belonging to a disadvantaged or oppressed community. Therefore, these youths may opt to stay closeted to avoid further pressures.

Disclosure

This is the point at which a lesbian or gay individual openly identifies his or her sexual orientation to another person. It is not appropriate to use terms such as discovered, admitted, revealed, found out, or declared to describe this event. These pejorative terms, which suggest judgement, should be avoided by professionals.

Being Out

This term describes a person who openly acknowledges their gay or lesbian sexual orientation to friends, family, colleagues, and society. Not everyone who is "out" is "out" among all of these groups. For instance, some people may be out to their family, but not to their colleagues at work.

Being Closeted or "In the Closet"

Someone who is not open about his or her sexual orientation is referred to as "being in the closet." This person, for personal reasons, chooses to hide his or her orientation from others. Some people may never "come out" to anyone other than themselves. Although there are great psychological consequences to be paid for doing so, it is possible for someone to stay in the closet even to himself or herself.

Heterocentrism

This is the assumption that everyone is heterosexual unless otherwise indicated. Heterocentrism is culturally, religiously, and socially motivated and is reinforced by most major institutions in American culture.

Homophobia

Developed by behavioral scientists, this term describes varying degrees of fear, dislike, and hatred of homosexuals or homosexuality. Such feelings may result in prejudice, discrimination, and hostile behavior toward people believed to be homosexual.

Homoignorant

This term describes individuals with limited knowledge about gays, lesbians, bisexual, and transgendered individuals.

Stigma

Stigma, defined as "a mark of shame or discredit" (Merriam Webster Collegiate Dictionary, 10th edition), is one factor that makes GLBTQ youth different from heterosexual youth. GLBTQ youth live with the knowledge that their identity as a GLBTQ person is stigmatized by society.

Culture-Specific Terms and Symbols

Reclaimed Negative Terms

Terms like bull dyke, fag, faggot, and queer (or maricon/maricona, or pato/patain in Spanish) are sometimes used to refer to lesbians and gay men in negative terms and are equivalent to hate terms and epithets used against racial and ethnic minorities. There is a political usage, however, for such words by some gays and lesbians who, in a reclamation process, redefine and use with pride words formerly used as pejorative terms. Because these words still carry a negative connotation in general society, their positive usage is restricted to lesbians and gay men who are active in the reclamation struggle. These terms are usually reserved for use by members of this group. Because they are "in-group words," you should not use them unless you are a member of these groups.

Lambda

Lambda (( ) is the eleventh letter of the Greek alphabet. Many gay men and lesbians use the lambda as a symbol that identifies their sexual orientation. Some lesbian/gay organizations use lambda in their names.

Pink Triangle

In Nazi Germany, persons identified as homosexuals were forced to wear the pink triangle and were then ostracized, persecuted, and killed by the Nazis. Gay men and lesbians have recently reclaimed the pink triangle as a symbol. They wear it as a badge of honor and also as a symbol of militancy against institutionalized oppression and denial of their civil rights in society.

Black Triangle

The black triangle is another recently reclaimed symbol that originated in Nazi Germany. There it was used to identify never-married women or women who did not bear children.

Intertwined Male Genetic Symbol

This variation of a traditional symbol (yy)identifies gay men.
Intertwined Female Genetic Symbol
This variation of a traditional symbol (xx) identifies lesbians.

Labarys

This symbol, a sacred double ax used by the ancient Amazons, has been reclaimed by modern lesbians as a sign of power.

Freedom Rings

Rainbow-colored, aluminum-oxidized rings worn on a chain around the neck are an outward symbol of gay and lesbian pride.

Rainbow Flag

A six-colored flag (red, orange, yellow, green, blue, purple) is a symbol of the gay and lesbian movement.

Stonewall Rebellion

Stonewall Inn on Christopher Street in New York City is the site where gays and lesbians fought with police for five days beginning on June 27, 1969. This event serves as the observed Independence

Day for gay and lesbian persons. While the Stonewall Rebellion is usually given as marking the start of the Gay and Lesbian Movement, two other liberation organizations actually preceded this event-The Mattachine Society (for gays) begun in 1950, and The Daughters of Bilitis (for lesbians) begun in 1955.

Resources

Printed Resources

Listed below are many books of interest to youth workers. Many journal articles, newspaper articles, and magazine articles could be added, but only books are listed due to space limitations. Additional books can be found through Internet searches and Internet retailers.

General GLBTQ Interest Books

Appleby, G., & Anastas, J. (1998). *Not just a passing phase.* New York: Columbia University Press.

Blumenfeld, W. J. (Ed.). (1992). *Homophobia: How we all pay the price.* Boston: Beacon Press.

Bornstein, K. (1995). *Gender outlaw: On men, women, and the rest of us.* New York: Vintage Books.

Brownworth,V. A. & Raffo, S. (1999). *Restricted access: Lesbians on disability.* Seattle, WA: Seal Press Feminist Publishing.

Clark, D. (1987). *Loving someone gay* (Revised). Berkeley: Celestial Arts.

D'Augelli, A. R. & Patterson, C. J. (Eds.). (1995). *Lesbian, gay, and bisexual identities over the lifespan.* New York: Oxford University Press.

Governor's Commission on Gay and Lesbian Youth. (1993). *Making schools safe for gay and lesbian youth: Breaking the silence in schools and in families.* Boston: Author. (Document is available in ERIC abstract link.)

Mallon, G. P. (Ed.). (1998). *Foundations of social work practice with lesbian and gay persons.* New York: Haworth Press.

Mallon, G. P. (Ed.). (1999). *Social services for transgendered youth.* New York: Haworth Press.

Marcus, E. (1993). Is it a choice? Answers to 300 of the most frequently asked questions about gays and lesbians. New York: HarperCollins Publications.

Pharr, S. (1988). *Homophobia: A weapon of sexism*. Little Rock, AR: Chardon Press.

Ratti, R. (Ed.). (1993). A lotus of another color: An unfolding of the South Asian gay and lesbian experience. Boston: Alyson Publishing.

Smith, B. (2000). *The truth that never hurts: Writings on races, genders, and freedom*. Piscataway, NJ: Rutgers University Press.

Books for and about GLBTQ Youth

Alyson, S. (Ed.). (1991). *Young, gay, and proud*. Boston: Alyson Publications.

Bauer, M. D. (Ed.). (1994). *Am I blue? Coming out from silence*. New York: HarperCollins Publications.

Children's Aid Society of Metropolitan Toronto. (1995). *We are your children too: Accessible child welfare services for lesbian, gay, and bisexual youth*. Toronto, ON: Author.

Child Welfare League of America. (1991). *Serving the needs of gay and lesbian youths: The role of child welfare agencies*. Washington, DC: Author.

Cohen, D., & Cohen, S. (1989). *When someone you know is gay*. New York: Dell.

DeCrescenzo, T. (Ed.). (1994). *Helping gay and lesbian youth: New policies, new programs, new practice*. New York: Haworth Press.

Feinberg, L. (1993). *Stone butch blues*. Boston: Firebrand Books.

Feinberg, L. (1996). *Transgender warriors*. Boston: Beacon Press.

Fricke, A. (1983). *Reflections of a rock lobster: A story about growing up gay*. Boston: Alyson Publications.

Harbeck, K. (Ed.). (1992). *Coming out of the classroom closet*. New York: Harrington Park Press.

Harris, M. B. (1998). *School experiences of gay and lesbian youth: The invisible minority*. New York: Haworth Press.

Herdt, G. (Ed.). (1988). *Gay and lesbian youth*. New York: Harrington Park Press.

Herdt, G., & Boxer, A. (1993). *Children of horizons: How gay and lesbian teens are leading the way out*. Boston: Beacon Press.

Heron, A. (Ed.). (1983). *One teenager in ten: Writings by gay and lesbian youth*. New York: Warner Books.

Heron, A. (Ed.). (1994). *Two in twenty*. Boston: Alyson Publications.

Jennings, K. (Ed.). (1994). *Becoming visible: A reader in gay and lesbian history for high school and college students*. Boston: Alyson Publications.

Kay, P., Estepa, A., & Desetta, A. (Eds.). (1996). *Out with it: gay and straight teens write about homosexuality*. New York: Youth Communications.

Mallon, G. P. (1998). *We don't exactly get the welcome wagon: The experiences of gay and lesbian adolescents in child welfare systems*. New York: Columbia University Press.

Mallon, G. P. (1999). *Let's get this straight: A gay and lesbian affirming approach to child welfare*. New York: Columbia University Press.

O'Brien, C. A., Travers, R., & Bell, L. (1993). *No safe bed: Lesbian, gay, and bisexual youth in residential services*. Toronto, ON: Central Toronto Youth Services.

Owen, R. E. (1998). *Queer kids: The challenges and promise for lesbian, gay, and bisexual youth*. New York: Haworth Press.

Remafedi, G. (Ed.). (1994). *Death by denial: Studies of suicide in gay and lesbian teenagers*. Boston: Alyson Press.

Ryan, K., & Futterman, D. (1998). *Lesbian and gay youth: Care and counseling*. New York: Columbia University Press.

Savin-Williams, R. C. (1998). *...And then I became gay*. New York: Routledge.

Schneider, M. (1988). *Often invisible: Counselling gay and lesbian youth*. Toronto, ON: Central Toronto Youth Services.

Schneider, M. (Ed.). (1997). *Pride and prejudice: Working with lesbian, gay, and bisexual youth*. Toronto, ON: Central Toronto Youth Services.

Scholinski, D. (1997). *The last time I wore a dress*. New York: Putnam.

Simpson, B. (1994). *Opening doors: Making substance abuse and other services more accessible to lesbian, gay, and bisexual youth*. Toronto, ON: Central Toronto Youth Services.

Singer, B.L. (Ed.). (1993). *Growing up gay/growing up lesbian: A literary anthology*. New York: The New Press.

Whitlock, K. (1989). *Bridges of respect* (2nd ed.). Philadelphia: American Friends Service Committee.

Books for Parents of GLBTQ Youth

Aarons, L. (1995). *Prayers for Bobby: A mother's coming to terms with the suicide of her gay son.* San Francisco: Harper.

Bernstein, R. A. (1995). *Straight parents, gay children: Keeping families together.* Boston: Thunder's Mouth Press.

Borhek, M. V. (1979). *My son Eric.* Cleveland, OH: Pilgrim Press.

Dew, M. F. (1994). *The family heart: A memoir of when our son came out.* Redding, MA: Addison-Wesley.

Fairchild, B., & Hayward, N. (1989). *Now that you know: What every parent should know about homosexuality* (Rev. edition). New York: Harcourt, Brace, Jovanovich.

Griffin, C. W., Wirth, M. J., & Wirth, A. (1986). *Beyond acceptance: Parents of lesbians and gays talk about their experiences.* Englewood Cliffs, NJ: Prentice-Hall.

Muller, A. (1987). *Parents matter.* Tallahassee, FL: Naiad Press.

Savin-Williams, R. (2001). *Mom, Dad, I'm gay.* Washington, DC: American Psychological Association.

Books for Gay, Lesbian, Bisexual, and Transgender People

Berzon, B. (Ed.). (1992). *Positively gay: New approaches to gay and lesbian life.* Berkeley: Celestial Arts.

Berzon, B. (1996). *Setting them straight: You can do something about bigotry and homophobia in your life.* New York: Plume/Penguin.

Borhek, M. (1993). *Coming out to parents.* Cleveland, OH: Pilgrim Press.

Bornstein, K. (1997). *My gender workbook.* New York: Routledge.

Hutchins, L., & Kaahumanu, L. (Eds.). (1991). *Bi any other name: Bisexual people speak out.* Boston: Alyson Publications.

Jensen, D., & Collasure, D. (2001). *Journey across the rainbow: Inspirational stories for the human race.* Boulder, CO: Rainbow Pride Press.

Monette, P. (1992). *Becoming a man: Half a life story.* New York: HarperCollins.

Preston, J. (Ed.). (1991). *Hometowns: Gay men write about where they belong.* New York: Penguin.

Raymond, D. (1985). *Looking at gay and lesbian life.* Boston: Beacon Press.

Sherman, P. (1994). *Uncommon heroes: A celebration of heroes and role models for gay and lesbian Americans.* New York: Fletcher Press.

Books Focusing on Human Sexuality

Bradley, L. J., Jarchow, E., Robinson, B., & Kottler, J. A. (1999). *All about sex: The school counselor's guide to handling tough adolescent problems.* New York: Corwin Press.

Carrera, M. (1991). *The language of sex: An A to Z guide.* New York: Facts on File, Inc.

Carrera, M. (1998). *The Wordsworth dictionary of sexual terms.* Lincolnwood, IL: NTC Publishing Group.

Publications for Professionals

Cass, V. C. (1979). Homosexual identity formation: A theoretical model. *Journal of Homosexuality, 4*(3), 219–235.

Coleman, E. (1987). Asessment of sexual orientation. *Journal of Homosexuality, 13*(4), 9–23.

DeMonteflores, C. & Schultz, S. J. (1978). Coming out: Similarities and differences for lesbians and gay men. *Journal of Social Issues, 34*(3), 59–72.

Garnets, L., Hancock, K. A., Cochran, S.D., & Peplau, A. (1991). Issues in psychotherapy with lesbians and gay men: A survey of psychologists. *American Psychologist, 46,* 964–972.

Kruks, G. (1991). Gay and lesbian homeless/street youth: Special issues and concerns. *Journal Adolescent Health, 12*(7), 515–518.

Le Vay, S. (1994). *The sexual brain.* Cambridge, MA: MIT Press.

Le Vay, S. (1997). *Queer science: The use and abuse of research on homosexuality.* Cambridge, MA: MIT Press.

Luna, G. C. (1991). Street youth: Adaptation and survival in the AIDS decade. *Journal of Adolescent Health, 12*(7), 511–514, 123.

Seattle Commission on Children and Youth. (1988). *Report on gay and lesbian youth in Seattle.* Seattle, WA: Seattle Commission on Children and Youth.

Troiden, R. R. (1993). The formation of homosexual identities. In L. D. Garnets and D. C. Kimmel (Eds.). *Psychological perspectives on lesbian and gay male experiences.* New York: Columbia University Press, pp. 191–217.

Victim Services/Traveler's Aid. (1991). *Streetwork project study.* New York: Victim Services.

National Magazines Featuring GLBTQ Topics and Interests

All the magazines listed below target audiences of both women and men, with the exception of *Curve* (formerly *Deneuve*).

The Advocate
"The national gay and lesbian news magazine"
P.O. Box 541
St. Morris, IL 61054-784
800/827-0561

Curve (formerly *Deneuve*)
"The lesbian magazine"
2336 Market Street, #25,
San Francisco, CA 94114
818/760-8983

Genre
A magazine for GLBTQ folks
P.O. Box 18449
Anaheim, CA 92817-8449
800/576-9933

Out
Features culture, media, politics, work, fashion, health
P.O. Box 1935
Marion, OH 43306-2035
800/876-1199

Venus
A magazine for people of African descent in "the life"
P.O. Box 150
Hastings-on-Hudson, NY 10706
914/376-6161

Academic Research Journals

Journal of Homosexuality
c/o Haworth Press
10 Alice Street
Binghamton, NY 13904-1580
800/342-9678

Journal of Gay and Lesbian Social Services
c/o Haworth Press
10 Alice Street
Binghamton, NY 13904-1580
800/342-9678

Recommended Videos

A beautiful thing. (1996). Two English teenagers live and learn about their gay identity. This film is excellent to use to generate discussion about family acceptance. Available for rental at local video stores. 89 min. (R).

The adventures of Priscilla, queen of the desert (1994). In this Australian comedy, a transsexual (Terence Stamp) and two drag queens travel to remote Outback locations to put on lip-synch performances. They and their pink bus, named Priscilla, get homophobic, bewildered responses in strong, politically incorrect language. ABBA fans will appreciate the music; critics have praised the acting and serious reflection on three stages of life. Directed by Stephan Elliott, written by and costarring Hugo Weaving. 103 min. (R).

Before Stonewall: The making of the gay and lesbian community. (1986). Materials and interviews trace the history of the lesbian and gay experience in the United States prior to 1969. Available from Cinema Guild, 1697 Broadway, New York, NY 10019; 212/246-5522.

Boys don't cry. (1999; also known as *Take it like a man*). Written and directed by Kimberly Pierce, this story is based on actual events. Brandon Teena is a popular new guy in a tiny Nebraska town, drinking, hanging out, and charming the young women. He has not mentioned that he is actually a woman, Teena Brandon. His life is torn apart by betrayal, humiliation, and violence. 118 min., (R).

But, I'm a cheerleader. (1999; also known as *Make me over*). Meagan is a cheerleader with a boyfriend. She doesn't like kissing him and has pictures of girls in her locker, so her parents and friends conclude she must be gay. They send her to a "sexual redirection" school to learn how to be straight. What she learns is the theme of this romantic comedy, written and directed by Jamie Babbit. 85 min. Two versions, (R) and (NC-17), are available in the U.S.

Choosing children: A film about lesbians becoming parents. (1985). This film is an intimate look at the issues faced by women who become parents after coming out as lesbians. Cambridge Documentary Films, P.O. Box 385, Cambridge, MA 02139; 617/354-3677.

Closets are health hazards. (1995). Sixteen lesbian and gay physicians discuss the medical profession and sexual orientation. The format is a slide show transferred to video. Woman Vision, c/o Transit Media, 22D Hollywood Avenue, Hohokus, NJ 07423; 800/343-5540.

Common threads: Stories from the quilt. (1989). Narrated by Dustin Hoffman, this Academy Award-winning video tells the stories of five people with AIDS, including an Olympic athlete, an 11-year-old suburban boy, and an urban married man. Available from commercial distributors.

Hate, homophobia, and schools. (1992). The title of this film reflects the theme. Copies can be obtained from Newist Studio B, IS 1040, University of Wisconsin, Green Bay, WI 54311; 414/ 465-2599.

Homoteens. (1995). These stories are mostly about urban youth of color who are gay, lesbian, and bisexual. The film can be obtained by contacting the distributor: Frameline, 346 Ninth Street, San Francisco, CA 94103; e-mail: frameline@aol.com

I just want to say. (1998). Using stories of young people in community-based school programs, this film explores the antigay climate that exists in most schools. It also offers suggestions for educators on how to improve the situation. The film can be purchased from GLSEN, 121 West 27th Street, New York, NY 10001; 212/727-0135.

The incredible true adventure of two girls in love. (1995). Written and directed by Maria Maggenti, this comedy is about two young women, Randy and Evie, from two different social and economic backgrounds. They find themselves in the typical struggles of a new romance. 91 min. (R).

Ma vie en rose (My life in pink) (1997). A brilliant film from Belgium about an 8-year-old transgender (male to female) child who insists on living life as a girl. Her family at first appears to be accepting, but they alter their response when external pressures are put upon them. This film can be rented at local video stores. French, English subtitles; 88 min. (R).

Out loud. (1995). This brief film (19 minutes) about GLBTQ youth can be obtained by contacting the distributor: Frameline, 346 Ninth Avenue, San Francisco, CA 94103; 414/703-8650.

Pink triangles. (1995). This documentary explores homophobia through interviews with people who have firsthand knowledge of discrimination. Available from: Cambridge Documentary Films, P.O. Box 385, Cambridge, MA 02139; 617/354-3677.

Sexual orientation: Reading between the labels. (1992). A broad overview on many of the important issues about sexual orientation, this film includes interviews with GLBTQ youth and their families. Contact: Newist Studio B, IS 1040, University of Wisconsin, Green Bay, WI 54311; 414/465-2599.

Silent pioneers: Gay and lesbian elders. (1985). These are the stories of eight individuals from diverse, regional, ethnic, racial, and professional backgrounds who lived through an era when homosexuality was tolerated. Contact: SAGE, Film Makers Library, 124 East 40th Street, #901, New York, NY 10016; 212/355-6545.

Straight from the heart. (1995). Parents talk about coming to terms with having a gay or lesbian child. Available from: Woman Vision, c/o Transit Media, 22D Hollywood Avenue, Hohokus, NJ 07423; 800/343-5540.

Tongues untied. (1989). This film describes the homophobia and racism that confront Black gay men. Contact: Wolfe Video, P.O. Box 64, New Alameda, CA 95042; 408/268-6782.

Twilight of the Golds. (1997). This commercially released film, starring Brendan Fraser and Faye Dunaway, highlights the internal and external struggles that families experience when dealing with the reality of having a gay family member. Available at local video stores. 92 minutes (PG-13).

Working it out: Scenes from the lives of lesbian, gay and bisexual youth. (1995). This film addresses the difficult issues that lesbian and gay adolescents face in the coming out process. Available from: HIV Center/RFMH, 722 West 168th Street, New York, NY 10032; 212/740-0046.

Internet Resources

Sexual Orientation: Science, Education, and Policy

Gender PAC is a political action committee (PAC) with the motto: "Gender rights are human rights." A national advocacy organization, GenderPAC works to insure all Americans' right to their gender free from stereotypes, discrimination, and violence, regardless of how they look, act, or dress, or how others perceive their sex or sexual orientation. GenderPAC is especially concerned with the way discrimination based on gender intersects with other kinds of discrimination, including race, class, ethnicity, and age. Check the website, www.gpac.org, for additional information.

The work of Gregory Herek, University of California at Davis, an authority on antigay prejudice, hate crimes, and the stigma of AIDS is featured on the website www.psychology.ucdavis.edu/rainbow/index.htm.. Factual information about sexual orientation is provided to promote the use of scientific knowledge for education and enlightened public policy. Information is included on homophobia, hate crimes, gays in the military, homosexuality and mental health, homosexuality and child molestation, and changing sexual orientation.

The Human Rights Campaign focuses on national political issues affecting GLBT Americans, including workplace discrimination, combating hate crimes, fighting HIV/AIDS, protecting our families, and working for better lesbian health. The website, www.hrc.org, features "how to" tools, news releases, National Coming Out Project resources, and information about topics including schools and higher education, adoption, aging, domestic partner agreements, money, and parenting.

Lambda Legal Defense and Education Fund is a national organization committed to achieving full recognition of the civil rights of lesbians, gay men, and people with HIV/AIDS through litigation, education and public policy work. Information on AIDS projects and other issues dealing with employment discrimination, same-sex marriage, the military ban, anti-gay initiatives, and foster care projects is found on the website at www.lambdalegal.org.

The National Gay and Lesbian Task Force works for the civil rights of GLBT people. NGLTF celebrates diversity of race, sexual orientation, gender identity, religion, ethnicity, age, disability, and income. Through the Policy

Institute and leadership development activities, NGLTF works closely with social justice organizations at the local, state, and national levels to address homophobia, racism, sexism, and all forms of discrimination. For more details, see the website: www.ngltf.org.

Parents, Families, and Friends of Lesbians and Gays (PFLAG) is a national organization dedicated to providing information, education, and support for the parents, families, and friends of lesbians and gays. A list of local chapters, the mission statement, and general information about sexual orientation are available on the PFLAG website: www.pflag.org.

Answers to Questions About Sexual Orientation and Homosexuality

The American Psychological Association (APA) website has a page on sexual orientation as well as APA Policy Statements on Lesbian, Gay, and Bisexual Concerns at www.apa.org/pubinfo/orient.html and pi/lgbpolicy/copy.html.

The Gay, Lesbian, and Straight Education Network (GLSEN) fights homophobia in grades K to12 in schools around the country. A wealth of information on gay and lesbian youth suicide as well as the effects of homophobia on our children is available on the website: www.glsen.org.

The primary goal of Lesbian and Gay Public Awareness Project (LGPAP) is to provide resources for people to educate others about the gay and lesbian community. An online version of their helpful brochure, *Homophobia: What are we so afraid of?*, is available at their website: www.swlink.net/~aware. This brochure is also available in Spanish from ARENAL, a LesbiGay homepage in Spanish at www.indiana.edu/~arenal/ingles.html or lindex.html in Spanish.

Planet Out offers news, advice, and information on travel, entertainment, education, and GLBT history on what is considered the largest and most popular commercial GLBT website, www.planetout.com. The GLBTQ online audience is estimated to be about 9 to 10 million persons worldwide. Planet Out also sponsors radio and television programs, 50 events a year, and 4 e-mail newsletters.

The Straight Spouse Network (SSSN) organization and website provide support and information for spouses (current and former) and the children of gays and lesbians. The website is www.glpci.org/~ssn.

Children of Lesbians and Gays Everywhere (COLAGE) is an organization for persons with lesbian, gay, bisexual, and transgendered parents. The website is www.colage.org.

Family Pride Coalition, an organization is for gay, lesbian, bisexual, and transgendered parents and their families, has a website at www.familypride.org.

My child is gay, an article by Barb Chandler, is posted on the Mental Health Net. The article is intended for parents who are dealing with the initial news that their child is gay or lesbian. The website is www.cmhc.com/perspective/articles/art05966.htm .

GLBT Youth and Youth Concerns

OutProud!, also known as the National Coalition for Gay, Lesbian, Bisexual, and Transgendered Youth, deals with lesbian and gay issues as they pertain to young people. A wide variety of resources for youth and educators are found on the website: www.outproud.org.

P.E.R.S.O.N. Project (Public Education Regarding Sexual Orientation Nationally) is a national and local activist network that advocates for inclusive curricula in public schools. Excellent current information is listed on the website: www.youth.org/loco/PERSONProject.

Resources for Parents of Gay, Lesbian, Bisexual, and Transgendered Youth

Excellent information for parents of GLBTQ youth and links to web pages of GLBTQ youth, advice, questions and answers, and resource identification are all found on www.pe.net/~bidstrup/parents.htm.

Youth and AIDS Project (YAP) helps to prevent HIV among high-risk youth and helps to care for young people and families living with HIV infection. The website is www/peds.umn.edu/Centers/YAP.

Youth Assistance Organization also called Youth Action Online; YAO) has a website that provides information for gay, lesbian, bisexual, and transgender youth and links to other sites. The site is www.youth.org.

Youth Suicide Problems: Gay and Bisexual Male Focus

A website that includes current studies and research findings on gay and bisexual male youth suicide is virtualcity.com/youthsuicide.

GLBTQ Organizations

Listed below are key GLBTQ or GLBTQ-affirming youth organizations in central locations throughout the United States and Canada. For a more extensive list of GLBTQ youth organizations in your local community, try looking at the website angelfire.com, or use the key words "gay and lesbian youth organizations" on any Internet search engine.

Boston Alliance of Gay and Lesbian Youth (BAGLY)

BAGLY is a youth-led, adult-supported social support organization for gay, lesbian, bisexual, transgendered, questioning youth, and their straight allies, age 22 and under. The organization is committed to providing a safe, healthy, nonexploitive, and supportive atmosphere in all its meetings, activities, special events, and programs. The group is also pressure free, violence free, weapons free, alcohol free, drug free, and sex free.

P.O. Box 814
Boston, MA 02103
617/227-4313
800/42-BAGLY (toll-free automated information line)
www.bagly.org

Central Toronto Youth Services (CTYS)
Lesbian, Gay, and Bisexual Youth Program

CTYS is a community-based Children's Mental Health Center committed to identifying and meeting the needs of high-risk and hard-to-serve youth, their families, and the youth-serving community. In keeping with its mandate of providing direct-service programming, education, and research, CTYS moved to bridge an important gap in social services for gay, lesbian, and bisexual youth by establishing the Sexual Orientation and Youth Program in 1983. Initially providing training and resources for social service providers working with lesbian, gay, and bisexual youth, the program has continually evolved. Since 1986, the program has published innovative research on issues relevant to lesbian, gay, and bisexual youth, as well as offered training and consultation to health and social service providers and educators. The program also offers direct care services: counseling, support, group services for GLBTQ youth and has an extensive array of publications.

e-mail: lgbyctys@interlog.com
65 Wellesley Street East, 3rd Floor

Toronto, Ontario M4Y 1G7
416/924-2100
www.interlog.com~lgbyctys/

Gay and Lesbian Adolescent Social Services (GLASS)

GLASS services are targeted for youth who are self-identified as gay, lesbian, bisexual; who are confused about their psychosexual identities; who are at risk of engaging in high-risk behaviors (such as prostitution, substance abuse, drug-dealing); who are at risk for abuse and exploitation (being sexually abused, pimped, turned-out); and who are at risk for HIV-infection. High-risk children and youth served by the agency are from diverse ethnic backgrounds, including African American, Hispanic, Asian/Pacific Islander, Native American, and White.

Although the agency's programs are uniquely designed for gay and lesbian as well as HIV-affected children, as the agency has grown, it has served (and continues to serve) all youngsters in need, regardless of sexual orientation. GLASS programs include 3 foster family agencies, 5 residential group homes with a total of 36 residents, and a Mobile Health Outreach Project for street youth.

650 Robertson Boulevard
West Hollywood, CA 90069
310/358-8727
310/358-8721 (fax)
www.home.glassLA.org/glass
email: glass@labridge.com

Gay, Lesbian, Straight Education Network (GLSEN)

Founded as a small volunteer group in Boston in 1990, GLSEN led the fight that made Massachusetts the first state to ban antigay discrimination in its public schools in 1993. GLSEN became a national organization in 1994 and has since built a network of 85 local chapters. A national office in New York, opened in 1995, and a Western Field office in San Francisco, opened in 1998, support these chapters. GLSEN is dedicated to ending the cycle of bigotry in educational systems by teaching the lesson of respect for all in public, private, and parochial schools, grades K to 12. GLSEN strives to assure that each member of every school community is valued and respected, regardless of sexual orientation.

21 West 27th Street
New York, NY 10001
212/727-0135, phone
212/727-0254, fax
www.glsen.org

Green Chimneys Children's Services

This agency represents diverse ethnic backgrounds, including African American, Hispanic, Asian, Native American, and white. Although the agency's programs are uniquely designed for GLBTQ as well as HIV-impacted children, it has served (and continues to serve) all youngsters in need, regardless of sexual orientation. Green Chimneys programs based in New York City include:

- The Audre Lorde High School for GLBTQ youth;
- The Gramercy Life Skills Residence for youth ages 16 to 20 (totaling 25 residents);
- The AOBH Program for 12 youth (6 gay, ages 12 to15; and 6 lesbian, ages 14 to17);
- Ten supervised independent living apartment programs for youth ages 18 to 21 (totaling 20 residents);
- Three supervised transitional living apartments for runaway and homeless GLBTQ youth ages 17 to 21 (totaling 8 residents);
- Triangle Tribe Training Services, a resource center for technical assistance, resource distribution and train

ing seminars for education, social services, health, and mental health professionals;

- Triangle Tribe Family Services, family support services and a mentoring program for families affected by issues related to sexual orientation.

456 West 145th Street, Suite 1
New York, NY 10032
212/491-5911
212/368-8975 (fax)
www.greenchimneys.org

National Network for Youth

The National Network for Youth is a 22-year-old membership organization with more than 400 direct members. With its regional and state network affiliates, the National Network for Youth represents over 1,200 constituents, primarily community-based youth-serving agencies. The mission of the National Network for Youth is to ensure that all young people can be safe and grow up to lead healthy and productive lives. A driving force for the National Network for Youth in achieving its mission is Community Youth Development (CYD). The National Network for Youth actively engages in public education efforts, promotes youth/adult partnerships, and strives to strengthen staff and community-based organization capacity to provide effective programs and services to youth in high-risk situations. Training and technical assistance are provided in a variety of areas, including professional development of youth workers, youth leadership, GLBTQ youth services, peer education, HIV/AIDS and substance abuse prevention, grant writing, and community and youth development.

1319 F Street, NW
Suite 401
Washington, DC 20004
202/783-7949
www.nn4youth.org

Parents and Friends of Gays and Lesbians (PFLAG)

PFLAG is a national nonprofit organization with a membership of over 70,000 households and more than 400 affiliates worldwide. This grassroots network has its national office in Washington, DC. PFLAG promotes the health and well-being of gay, lesbian, bisexual, and transgender persons as well as their families and friends through support, to cope with an adverse society; education, to enlighten an ill-informed public; and advocacy, to end discrimination and to secure equal civil rights. PFLAG provides an opportunity for dialogue about sexual orientation and gender identity and takes action to create a society that is healthy and respectful of human diversity.

1101 14th Street, NW, Suite 1030
Washington, DC 20005
202/638-4200
202/638-0243 (fax)
www.pflag.org

Project 10

Project 10 is an on-site counseling program organized in 1984 to meet the needs of adolescent lesbians/gays in the educational system. Begun at Fairfax High School in Los Angeles, Project 10 has become a model program in other school districts. The focus of the model is education, reduction of verbal and physical abuse, suicide prevention, and accurate AIDS information. Project 10 is committed to keeping students in school, off drugs, and sexually responsible through providing accurate information and nonjudgmental counseling on issues of sexual orientation. Project 10 also benefits the non-gay population through public education and teaching youth how to live peacefully in an increasingly diverse society. Project 10 services include workshops and training sessions for administrators and staff, informal drop-in counseling at school sites, outreach to parents and significant others, liaison with peer counseling, substance abuse and suicide prevention programs, and coordination with health education programs that encourage sexual responsibility and risk-reduction. Recent special projects include the Models of Pride Conference, the Models of Excellence Scholarship Program, the Gay and Lesbian Youth Prom, Youth Lobby Day, and Administrative Training Seminars.

2955 South Robertson Boulevard
Los Angeles, CA 90034
626/577-4533
310/815-1744 (fax)
www.project10.org

Sexual Minority Youth Assistance League (SMYAL)

SMYAL is a youth service agency serving the Washington DC metropolitan area, including Maryland and Northern Virginia. The mission is to support and enhance the self-esteem of sexual minority youth, i.e., any youth (ages 13 to 21) who are lesbian, gay, bisexual, transgendered, or may be questioning their sexuality, and to increase public awareness and understanding of their issues. SMYAL works to increase the scope and quality of its services and to provide a safer future for youth who self-identify as gay, for youth questioning their sexual orientation, and for their friends and families.

410 7th Street, SE
Washington, DC 20003-2707
202/544-1306 (fax)
202/546-7796 (TTY)
www.smyal.org

Youth and AIDS Project (YAP)

The University of Minnesota YAP was founded in 1989. Its mission is to prevent transmission of HIV to and from high-risk youth and to provide care to youth and families living with HIV infection. The governing philosophy is that adolescents can and do make responsible health-related decisions if they are given appropriate resources and support. YAP programs are grounded in the belief that, to be effective, HIV-related services for youth must be developmentally appropriate, culturally competent, coordinated, and family-centered. YAP adheres to a "one-stop shopping" model of care, offering the most commonly needed services at a single agency, with convenient appointments and minimal waiting times. All grant-supported services are free to clients who can easily meet various needs or transition between the different levels of care in a familiar environment, with a continuity of caregivers. Centralized services also enable appointments to be scheduled at families' convenience and reduce logistical and administrative barriers to care.

428 Oak Grove Street
Minneapolis, MN 55403
612/627-6820
612/627-6819 (fax)
www.peds.umn.edu/Centers/YAP

About the Author

Gerald P. Mallon, DSW, is Associate Professor and the Director of the National Resource Center for Foster Care and Permanency Planning at Hunter College School of Social Work. His research interests focus on the experiences of gay and lesbian children, youth, and families within the context of child welfare service delivery. Dr. Mallon is the author of *We Don't Exactly Get the Welcome Wagon: The Experiences of Gay and Lesbian Adolescents in Child Welfare Systems* (Columbia Press, 1998) and *Let's Get This Straight: A Gay and Lesbian Approach to Child Welfare* (Columbia Press, 2000). He is also editor of *Foundations of Social Work Practice with Gay and Lesbian Persons* (Haworth Press, 1998) and *Social Services for Transgender Youth* (Haworth Press, 1999).

Correspondence may be sent to: 129 East 79th Street, New York, New York 10021 or via e-mail to mrengmal@aol.com.